ASSETIZATION

ASSETIZATION

SECOND EDITION

INSIDE THE **TRILLION-DOLLAR** INVESTING REVOLUTION

PATRICK LOEPFE | PHILIPPE A. NAEGELI | TOM LYONS

WILEY

Registered Office(s)
John Wiley & Sons, Inc., 111 River Street, Hoboken, NJ 07030, USA
John Wiley & Sons Ltd, New Era House, 8 Oldlands Way, Bognor Regis, West Sussex, PO22 9NQ, UK
John Wiley & Sons Singapore Pte. Ltd, 134 Jurong Gateway Road, #04-307H, Singapore 600134

For details of our global editorial offices, customer services, and more information about Wiley products visit us at www.wiley.com.

The manufacturer's authorized representative according to the EU General Product Safety Regulation is Wiley-VCH GmbH, Boschstr. 12, 69469 Weinheim, Germany, email: Product_Safety@wiley.com.

Library of Congress Cataloging-in-Publication Data is Available:

ISBN 9781394401765 (Cloth)
ISBN 9781394401789 (ePub)
ISBN 9781394401772 (ePDF)

Cover Design: Wiley
Author Photos: Courtesy of Patrick Loepfe, Courtesy of Philippe Naegeli, Courtesy of Tom Lyons

Set in 11/16pt, MinionPro by Straive, Chennai, India.
Printed and bound by CPI Group (UK) Ltd, Croydon, CR0 4YY

C9781394401765_130426

Generative AI Disclosure

The AI tools Claude Sonnet (4.5), Claude Opus (4.5), ChatGPT (5.0-5.2, Standard, Thinking and Pro versions), Perplexity (various models), and NotebookLM were used to support the creation of this book as declared below. Grammarly, including its AI functions, was used for copywriting and initial copyediting. These are collectively referred to as the "AI models" in the disclosure below. The use of AI is intended to be in alignment with the disclosure and declaration guidance in Wiley's Author FAQs.

Generative AI Use in Research Analysis

The AI models assisted in analyzing author interviews and related research materials. The AI helped identify and summarize primary and secondary sources, identify recurring themes, analyze data, and test conclusions. All AI-generated analyses were validated against original research data.

Generative AI Use in Content Development

Initial drafts were developed with assistance from the AI models, in particular those from Claude. All content was thoroughly reviewed by the authors and where needed revised for accuracy, completeness, and clarity. Grammarly was used specifically for language refinement and generating alternative examples, with all suggestions selectively incorporated based on subject matter expertise.

Generative AI Use in Content Analysis

The AI models were employed for analyzing potential gaps in coverage and redundant content. The AI helped identify where similar topics appeared across multiple chapters and suggested areas needing additional coverage based on the research findings. All gap analysis and redundancy recommendations were reviewed and validated before making content adjustments.

Generative AI Use in Review Process

The AI models were used to analyze drafts for clarity, consistency, and potential gaps in coverage. This AI-assisted review complemented human expert review carried out by the authors. All AI feedback was evaluated and selectively incorporated based on human judgment.

Patrick would like to dedicate this book to the memory of his father, who passed away shortly before GenTwo was founded and so could not witness the birth of assetization.

Philippe would like to dedicate this book to his wife Ramiza without whom it, as so much else, could never have happened—"Thanks for letting me win!"

Tom would like to dedicate this book to his mother, his first hero.

CONTENTS

CONTENTS

CONTENTS

Contents

FOREWORD BY JIM WIANDT, FOUNDER OF ETF.COM

The arc of modern investing has always bent toward greater access, greater transparency, and greater investor empowerment. Yet every few decades, a technology or structural shift emerges that doesn't simply improve the system, it rewires it. Exchange-traded funds were one of those shifts. When I founded ETF.com, I witnessed firsthand how a simple, elegant wrapper could demystify markets, collapse costs, and bring institutional-grade investing to anyone with a brokerage account. ETFs transformed how the world builds portfolios because they transformed who held the power.

As I read *Assetization*, I am struck by the unmistakable sense that we are standing at the threshold of the next such transformation. And once again, the catalyst is a shift in power—away from centralized manufacturers of financial products and toward the people who actually use them.

For the authors, Patrick, Philippe, and Tom, *assetization* is the process by which assets of all kinds—traditional, private, esoteric, digital, even imaginative—become investible, customizable, and ultimately securitized in ways that anyone can access. In other words, assetization picks up exactly where the ETF revolution left off.

ETFs cracked open the public markets. Assetization aims to crack open *everything else.*

THE ETF REVOLUTION WAS ONLY THE BEGINNING

To understand assetization, you have to appreciate just how monumental the ETF innovation was. ETFs did not win because they were "passive." They won because they transferred decision-making power from product issuers to investors. Suddenly individuals could build portfolios with surgical precision—tilting to regions, industries, factors, or themes. ETFs gave investors choice, and with choice came control.

This was the beginning of **Wave 1**, as this book describes it: the transition from a sellers' market to a buyers' market. Investors no longer relied on fund companies to conceive, construct, and deliver the perfect product. Investors could mix and match exposures like building blocks.

But as powerful as ETFs are, their reach is limited. They play almost entirely within the 17% of global economic activity represented by public markets. The remaining 83%—private assets, alternatives, intellectual property, revenue streams, niche opportunities, and the long tail of personal or passion-based assets—remains locked away behind walls of regulation, illiquidity, or structural complexity.

The core insight of *Assetization* is that the hunger for these assets is already visible everywhere. Investors want meaning-driven portfolios. They want diversification beyond stocks and bonds. They want to invest in what they care about, from innovative private companies driving change to art and music or local real estate opportunities.

But the system still tells them: *"You can only choose from what we've built for you."*

Assetization is what happens when that answer becomes unacceptable.

CONTAINERIZATION: THE TURNING POINT

In **Wave 2**—the containerization of finance—the authors show how the infrastructure of product creation is being transformed in ways that resemble the shipping revolution of the 1950s. Standardized containers didn't just move goods more efficiently; they rewired global trade. Similarly, securitization and tokenization frameworks are evolving into standardized "containers" for investment exposures of all kinds.

This is the frontier where the team at GenTwo have been operating: building infrastructure that makes it possible to wrap almost any economic exposure—yield streams, private assets, strategies, even idiosyncratic opportunities—into investible, compliant, transferable products.

This removes the bottleneck that has constrained innovation for decades: only the sell-side could manufacture products. Investors could choose from the menu, but not design the kitchen.

Containerization dissolves that barrier.

When financial professionals—and eventually individuals—can create products as easily as they curate them, the very definition of a "financial product" changes. Advisors and investors move from distributors to architects. Investors move from consumers to co-creators. Entire categories of inaccessible assets become investible.

To someone who lived through the early ETF years, this feels familiar. But it's also more radical. ETFs democratized access to public markets. Assetization democratizes access to *wealth creation itself.*

FROM PROMPT TO PRODUCT: WAVE 3 AND THE UNIMAGINABLE FUTURE

Wave 3 is where the authors' vision becomes extraordinary. If Waves 1 and 2 were about democratizing access and creation, Wave 3 is about democratizing *imagination.* AI-enabled platforms will soon allow users to design investment products through natural language—"I want a product that captures early-stage clean-tech innovations with downside protection"—and the entire value chain, from structuring to issuance to distribution, will be automated.

The cost of creation approaches zero. The friction evaporates. The boundaries between the buy side and the sell side dissolve entirely.

For anyone who watched ETFs take the world from a handful of index funds to thousands of thematic, factor, and niche exposures, this next step is not far-fetched—it is inevitable, and it is thrilling.

THE FUTURE IS WIDER THAN WE THINK

When I look back at the early days of ETFs, the magnitude of what they ultimately enabled wasn't obvious at first. But the pattern is unmistakable: when technology expands what can be securitized, the entire investment universe expands with it.

Assetization is the next expansion.

This book is a map of that future—clear-eyed, ambitious, and grounded in real industry transformation. Whether you're an advisor, allocator, founder, or investor, this is not simply a book about where finance is going. It's a book about the tools you will soon have in your hands.

And if history is any guide, once investors have access to better tools, the world changes.

Assetization is that change. And it is only just beginning.

PREFACE

There is a revolution happening in the investment industry. We call it assetization, and it will reshape how people invest and how financial products get made. In our opinion, it also represents a once-in-a-generation opportunity for investors, independent financial advisors, and institutional wealth managers. If you fall into one of these three categories, this book is for you.

For generations, investing has meant public markets. Most investors have been confined to listed securities—stocks, bonds, mutual funds, ETFs—and have had to settle for whatever products the industry chose to put on the shelf. Advisors and wealth managers, meanwhile, have been stuck with a narrow toolset, unable to build truly custom solutions even when they could see exactly what their clients needed. This is no longer good enough.

Public markets are vast, but they are also limited. They represent a relatively narrow slice of the real economy, and that slice is shrinking as fewer companies go public. At the same time, traditional products ignore enormous categories of assets: private equity and venture capital, infrastructure, real estate, private credit, digital assets, and "passion" and frontier assets such as art, collectibles, and tokenized data. The majority of the world's wealth sits outside the universe most portfolios can reach.

It is no surprise that investors and their advisors want more—more asset choices, more control, and solutions that reflect what people actually believe and care about rather than what happens to be available.

The good news is that this is changing.

Over the past 10 years, we have seen the barriers to private markets and other alternative investments begin to come down. New marketplaces are making it easier for people to access investments that were previously out of reach. New types of assets, from cryptocurrencies to collectibles, are going mainstream. New platforms and products are providing hands-on investors with the tools to create their own portfolios.

We see this democratization of access as the first wave of assetization. As the investment industry works to bring previously inaccessible assets into the investment universe, the old "seller's market" of investment products, controlled by large institutions that decide what products get made, is shifting into a "buyer's market," characterized by low costs and greater choice.

But this is only the beginning. The tip of the iceberg.

The upcoming democratization of financial product creation will be far more interesting and potentially transformative. Thanks to new technologies, innovative approaches, and the ongoing disaggregation of the financial product value chain, it is becoming easier than ever to create and issue financial products across all types of assets. This process shifts control away from large financial institutions with their massive product factories and into the hands of independent financial advisors, wealth managers, multi-family offices, and others who are closer to investors and better attuned to their needs. This will benefit their clients significantly. By breaking the quasi-monopoly on financial product creation, this wave of assetization will also level the playing field in the industry. Smaller or independent players who leverage these tools effectively will be able to enhance their offerings, differentiate themselves from competitors, and stand their ground against the dominant incumbents currently shaping the landscape.

As importantly, this wave will unlock trillions of dollars of value by opening up assets that barely touch today's public markets. Hundreds of trillions of dollars in real estate, investible private companies, and infrastructure projects; trillions in art and collectibles; not to mention unknown quantities of new frontier assets like tokenized data or future cash flows, are all assetizable. Even a small fraction of that would represent a generation-defining opportunity for investors to access, shape, and share in value that was previously out of reach.

But it doesn't end there. We believe that the process of assetization will ultimately lead to the complete automation of the product creation value chain. Everything—from generating an idea for a product to researching, structuring, issuing it, and managing its lifecycle—will be automated and accessible through a platform or even an app. The entire marketing and distribution process will also be automated, brought together in digital marketplaces that connect sellers with investors worldwide.

For investors, the message of this book is clear: you no longer have to settle for portfolios built only from what happens to be on the shelf. Over time, assetization will allow you to invest in your beliefs—to express what you actually think, know, and care about through the assets you hold and the products you choose. For advisors and wealth managers, it offers a path to move from curator to creator, using new tools and structures to design solutions that truly fit your clients instead of forcing clients into prepackaged molds. For institutions and wealth management firms, it is an invitation to embrace these capabilities, bring them inside the organization, and use them to strengthen client relationships and hold on to assets.

This book is written from a practitioner's standpoint. We are not market analysts. We are not academics. We are builders. Our company, GenTwo, is dedicated to expanding the investment universe by building tools to democratize how financial products get made. This is an important part of the puzzle, but it is far from the only one. Assetization is unfolding on many levels and across many institutions at once. Our goal in these pages is simply to give that transformation a name, to sketch its main contours as clearly as we can, and to invite you to think about what it will mean for your own investing decisions, your clients, and your business.

This is a completely new world. The world of assetization.

HOW TO READ THIS BOOK

This book is addressed to investors and those who advise them. While it may seem like these are two clearly distinct groups—investors who buy financial products, advisors and wealth managers who sell them—in reality both groups are "consumers" of financial products. Investors use the products, their advisors, broadly stated, help them to find the right ones.

That said, assetization has different implications depending on which side you are on (though as a professional advisor you will likely be an investor too). To help, in Chapter 2 we introduce three personas: Ada the investor, Barbara the independent advisor, and Clark the institutional wealth manager. Throughout the book these characters reappear as proxies for you the reader in whichever role you feel applies to you. It is our intention that when Ada appears, she should stand for you as an investor. When Barbara or Clark do, they stand for you as a financial professional. In this way we hope to make the relevance of our arguments to you as clear as we can.

WHAT YOU WILL FIND INSIDE

This book is divided into two parts.

PART I: THE ASSETIZATION REVOLUTION

Chapter 1: It Will Never Work! We begin with our personal journey, launching GenTwo in a Zurich nightclub to a skeptical audience who told us "it will never work." We introduce the fundamental problem that motivated us: the friction inherent in traditional securitization that keeps vast amounts of global value locked away. This chapter lays the groundwork for the concept of "assetization"—not just as a technical fix for banking infrastructure, but as a broader movement to democratize the creation of financial products and radically expand the investment universe.

Chapter 2: The Buy Side and Its Discontents Here we introduce Ada, Barbara, and Clark—the three personas mentioned above that represent the modern investor, the independent advisor, and the institutional wealth manager. Through their eyes, we explore the "buy side's" growing discontent with the status quo: shrinking public markets, rising asset correlation, and a generic product shelf that no longer meets the needs of a younger, digital-native generation. We argue that the pressure from these dissatisfied stakeholders is the primary force driving the industry toward assetization.

Chapter 3: Wave 1—The Democratization of Access This chapter defines the first wave of assetization: the democratization of *access*. We trace the industry's shift from a "seller's market," where institutions dictate the menu, to a "buyer's market" defined by unprecedented choice. We look at how public and private markets are converging, and how new platforms and DIY tools are empowering investors to build their own playlists of assets. However, we note a critical limitation: while investors can now *buy* more products, they still rely on large institutions to *create* them.

Chapter 4: Wave 2—The Containerization of Finance We explore the second wave: the democratization of *creation*. Drawing on the history of the shipping container, we show how the infrastructure of finance is being standardized and modularized. Starting with securitization and tokenization as efficient "containers" for value, we demonstrate how the complex machinery of product creation is being disaggregated. This shift breaks the institutional monopoly on issuance, allowing independent players to use these tools to build their own financial products.

Chapter 5: Wave 3—Radical Automation We look ahead to the third and most radical wave: the full automation of the product lifecycle. Using a futuristic vignette set in an art gallery, we illustrate a "prompt-to-product" world where AI agents handle structuring, legal, and compliance in seconds. We predict a future where investment marketplaces become universal, the distinction between buy side and sell side dissolves, and almost any verifiable value—from art collections to industrial machinery—can be seamlessly turned into an investible asset.

Chapter 6: From Curator to Creator Returning to the present, we discuss what this infrastructure shift means for wealth managers and advisors right now. We argue that assetization offers a solution to the "middleman squeeze" by allowing advisors to evolve from mere curators of other people's products into creators of their own unique solutions. We outline how this shift helps professionals like Barbara and Clark differentiate their brands, protect their margins, and serve their clients with true personalization.

Chapter 7: Untapped Assets: The Trillion-Dollar Opportunity of Assetization We attempt to quantify the sheer scale of the assetization opportunity. Moving beyond the shrinking world of stocks and bonds, we tour the vast landscape of "untapped" value, including private equity, private credit, infrastructure, real estate, and passion assets. By providing rough estimates of these markets, we show that the majority of the world's wealth sits outside the public exchanges, waiting for the right infrastructure to unlock hundreds of trillions of dollars in investible value.

Chapter 8: Assetization and the History of Finance We place assetization in its historical context to show why this transformation is not a fad, but a continuation of financial history. By tracing the democratization of finance from the invention of joint-stock companies to the rise of ETFs and the internet, we demonstrate a consistent pattern: technology always drives markets toward lower friction and broader participation. Assetization is simply the next logical step in this centuries-long trajectory of financial evolution.

Chapter 9: Invest in Your Beliefs We conclude with a simple invitation: invest in your beliefs. Portfolios need no longer be constrained by what happens to be on the shelf; people can build portfolios that reflect what they actually think, know, and care about. Advisors need no longer be squeezed in the middle but instead can use assetization tools to become true creators of products and solutions, differentiating themselves in the market and strengthening their businesses. Institutional wealth managers can advocate to bring these capabilities inside their organizations to help ensure that client needs are truly met, and client assets stay put.

PART II: ASSET RUSH—TALES FROM THE ASSETIZATION FRONTIER

In the second part of the book, we hand the microphone to the pioneers on the front lines. This section features conversations with innovators across the spectrum—from crypto veterans to academic researchers to experts in carbon markets, fine art, and sports finance. These "tales from the frontier" provide real-world evidence of how assetization is currently reshaping the rails of finance, offering diverse perspectives on the challenges and massive potential of this shift.

ABOUT THE AUTHORS

Patrick Loepfe is a structured product and banking specialist, with more than 25 years of working experience in investment banking. His extraordinary mathematical and technological skills led him to be a key figure in Switzerland's fintech industry. Patrick was the mastermind and driving force behind Vontobel's Deritrade—a disruptive business model for distributing structured products. He founded his own company, d-struct AG, in 2015 and became a leading independent advisor to banks and financial product issuers on electronic structured products distribution strategy and process optimization. Patrick founded GenTwo in 2018 along with Philippe A. Naegeli, and is the Chairman of the company.

Philippe A. Naegeli is an experienced business leader and active investor with an over 30-year career in investment and merchant banking, management, and corporate governance. In 2007, he founded PAN Asset Management, where he established and led an international network of financial institutions and investment funds. In 2014, he was appointed CEO, Managing Partner, and Vice President of the Board of Forstmann & Co. USA, a financial institution that builds partnerships and value chains together with industry leaders, philanthropists, governmental, and non-governmental organizations to support entrepreneurs. Philippe co-founded GenTwo in 2018 with Patrick Loepfe, and is the company CEO.

Tom Lyons is a 30-year veteran of corporate communications with deep expertise in financial services, fintech, and emerging technologies. Born and raised in New York and educated at Columbia University, he moved to Zurich in 1994 where he worked in communications at Clariden Bank, Credit Suisse, and UBS. In 2014 he founded Lyons Communications, a boutique agency serving Swiss blue chips, SMEs, and technology startups. Tom became involved in blockchain in 2016, and has held roles at the Crypto Valley Association, Consensys, and the Enterprise Ethereum Alliance, among others. He has been with GenTwo since 2023, where he is responsible for the company's communications and thought leadership efforts.

Jim Wiandt (Foreword) is a longtime pioneer in the ETF space. He founded ETF.com (originally IndexUniverse.com), launched the print magazines *Journal of Indexes* and *ETFR* and the data business of ETFs.com as well as the influential global conference series Inside ETFs. He authored the book *Exchange Traded Funds* (2001) and helped popularize ETF research and education for advisors and investors. Today he serves as an Industry Partner in Stack Asset Management's Markets & Wealth venture capital fund.

PART I

THE ASSETIZATION REVOLUTION

In Part I of this book, we make our case that the investment industry is undergoing a fundamental structural shift—one that changes who can create financial products, what can become investible, and how portfolios get built.

This matters whether you're an investor frustrated by the gap between what you want to own and what's actually available, an advisor squeezed between fee pressure and commoditized products, or a wealth manager watching assets drift to competitors who can offer what you cannot.

We also try to answer the "so what?" question. We quantify the opportunity (trillions in previously inaccessible assets), explain why this is happening now (technology and market forces converging), and outline what it means for you as an investor, independent advisor, or wealth manager.

By the end of Part I, you'll understand not just what assetization is, but why it represents the most significant infrastructure shift in investing since the rise of ETFs—and what you can do about it.

The question isn't whether this transformation will happen. As Part II will show, it's already underway. The question is whether you'll help shape it or simply adapt to it after others have.

CHAPTER ONE

IT WILL NEVER WORK!

W hile this book is about the investment industry in general, not our company, the ideas and insights are rooted in our work here at GenTwo. For this reason, we thought it would make sense in the opening chapter to tell readers a bit about who we are and the background of the idea we would come to call assetization. In the chapters that follow we leave our company behind to look at assetization in general, along with what it means for you and the investment industry at large.

OUT OF STEALTH MODE

Our story begins on a summer night in 2018, as two of our authors, Patrick and Philippe, are about to be invited on stage at one of Zurich's premier nightclubs to announce the launch of their new business. They are not the main event that night. The club has been rented out to celebrate the

10th anniversary of one of Switzerland's premier structured products bro-kerages, a company with which Patrick and Philippe's fledgling startup will be partnering.

Nonetheless, they are more than a bit nervous. The atmosphere in the club, with its lush interiors and velvety décor, is electric, but also daunting. The room is filled to bursting with peers from the Swiss financial services community, most of whom are probably not expecting to see them up there that night—and all of whom, they are sure, will be surprised by what they have to say.

They are excited as well.

After a year of hard work building the company they call GenTwo, it feels good to be coming out of stealth mode to tell the world what they have been up to. In hindsight, the setting could not have been more appropriate for the launch of a new fintech company.

The club was located in the Seefeld area of Zurich, near the lake and the river Limmat. A ten-minute tram ride takes you to Paradeplatz and the heart of the Swiss financial center, putting them just downstream of the great Swiss banks and the country's long-established financial community, steeped in centuries of tradition and convention.

But being in Seefeld also means they are close to a tradition of creative disruption. At the end of his life, the pioneering modernist Irish writer James Joyce lived just around the corner from the club and is buried in a local cemetery up the hill. The avant-garde Dada movement started in the Cabaret Voltaire café, a short walk away. And Carl Jung, the revolutionary Swiss psychologist and psychiatrist, trained at the Burghölzli clinic, just 15 minutes away by car down the lake.

Not that Patrick or Philippe would ever consider themselves on the same level as those giants. But their work up to that point had convinced them that big changes were coming to the investment industry, and that they and others like them were onto something revolutionary—something that could significantly transform investing and, in its own way, the world.

TOOLMAKERS

To understand why they thought that way, you need to know something about Patrick and Philippe's history.

Patrick began in mathematics, attracted to the discipline's way of breaking problems down to their core. He was also intrigued by how abstract thinking could lead to practical solutions. His career took him from derivatives trading through financial engineering and process optimization to becoming the creator of Bank Vontobel's Deritrade platform, one of the first fully automated multi-issuer platforms for structured products in the world.

As he often says, he is the type of person who gets bored easily. When he worked as a trader, he was always inventing things to make his life easier—and many of those inventions ended up being used by others. For example, he developed a framework to retrieve pre-market stock prices, which was considered impossible at the time. Later, when he moved into structured products at Vontobel, he noticed how many manual processes were involved and believed there had to be a better way. So he and his boss sat down, bought some books on programming and SQL, and figured out how to automate many of the tasks their salespeople were doing. That experience planted the seeds for Deritrade. This theme has followed him throughout his career: finding ways to make things easier and more efficient. Once he has achieved that, he tends to move on to new challenges. He enjoys being a pioneer.

Philippe's path was different. He grew up in a banking family, absorbing the rhythms of the industry from an early age. He was never an academic like Patrick. Instead, he had a gift for connecting people and building relationships. He also speaks his mind. Once, after a heated exchange with American hedge fund pioneer Tony Forstmann, he was surprised to be offered the role of CEO of Forstmann's family office. What had seemed like bluntness turned out to be the kind of candor that earns trust.

Philippe takes pride in his ability to adapt quickly and learn fast. He considers himself lucky to have had many people around him from whom he could learn. His father, for example, taught him everything about banking, trust, and the financial industry, and was always a source of motivation.

Yet there is one major thing that Patrick and Philippe have in common: a desire to create tools that help others make a difference. Had they lived during the Gold Rush, GenTwo would have been a company selling shovels, not a securitization platform. Both men share a passion for giving people the tools to make things happen.

"Had they lived during the Gold Rush, GenTwo would have been a company selling shovels."

The two had known each other from the Zurich securities trading scene, sometimes as rivals on opposite ends of a trade. Years later, they met again at a wedding. Patrick had been thinking about a new venture. Having learned from his experience creating Deritrade, which helped democratize the creation of structured products, he believed the same could be applied to financial products more broadly. He explained it to Philippe, who immediately saw its potential. Soon after, they decided to team up. The result was the founding of GenTwo.

RETHINKING SECURITIZATION

So, what exactly were they doing?

The goal from the outset was to democratize the creation of financial products through a new approach to securitization. Securitization is the practice of packaging assets into investible financial products or "securities," typically to facilitate financing or create liquidity for illiquid assets.

It has been around for a long time and has been very successful. By transforming illiquid assets into tradable securities, it has made more types of investible assets available to more kinds of investors and provided new avenues for companies to raise capital. The problem is that, up to now, securitization has been the purview of large banks or specialist firms. It is generally costly and complex to accomplish and has traditionally been limited to high-volume transactions or fairly standardized underlying assets. In a nutshell, there is a lot of friction.

GenTwo set out to change this by rethinking the process and remixing the ingredients that go into it in order to remove that friction, make the tools of securitization available to a much larger clientele, and make the process efficient enough to be applied to any asset at almost any volume.

This was potentially revolutionary for a number of reasons. The most important of these is probably diversification. Harry Markowitz, the Nobel laureate American economist, famously said that "diversification is the only free lunch in investing." What he meant is that the more varied the investment opportunities you have, particularly the more uncorrelated assets, the better the risk-adjusted returns of a portfolio can be.

Yet, as Patrick and Philippe saw, many wealth managers and investors at the time found the available options frustratingly limited. People felt stuck in the world of traditional, bankable investments and hampered by the limits of the traditional banking system: limits on the kinds of products available, limits on access to many of the more interesting opportunities and, frankly, limits to the imagination of many financial services providers. Above all, there was, in their view, an overly constrained idea of what could be considered an asset and where potential value might be hiding.

But what if it did not have to be that way? What if, with a mix of creative thinking, innovative financial engineering, technology, and hard work, you could create a platform and a network to provide even the smallest asset managers with the tools to turn any asset or creative investment strategy into a bankable security? And do so in a fully compliant way, using well-known, standard financial instruments, but without the high costs, high-volume requirements, and constraints of using a bank for asset securitization? These were the kinds of questions they asked themselves as they conceived and started building the platform, and the answers had started to form in their minds.

Such a platform would give both asset managers and their clients more freedom, more choice, and so more chances for creativity and diversification. And if all the products were fully asset-backed, as in their approach they would be, it could dramatically reduce counterparty credit risk as well.

These would all be great things, but there was more. As they and their clients were aware, there is a whole universe of assets that at the time were hard, if not impossible, for most investors to access: things like private equity or hedge fund shares, or high-value tangible assets like art or fine wine. The kind of radically simple, efficient, and independent means of securitization they were espousing could be used as a key to unlock the door to these assets as well.

PUSHBACK

As Philippe and Patrick would discover on that opening night in Zurich, to which we now return, not everybody would share their enthusiasm or believe in this vision.

While Patrick and Philippe waited in the wings, the host of the evening—the CEO of the structured products brokerage firm—was on stage. In its first 10 years, his company had become the largest structured products broker in Switzerland, helping clients issue their own custom products by working with banks and other specialized issuers. Many representatives of those banks and issuers, whose support had fueled the firm's success, were in the audience that night.

Then the CEO started talking about the future. He said the company wanted to do more for its clients and planned to build its own issuance platform and become its own issuer, bypassing the banks it had relied on before. That grabbed the crowd's attention, and the room quieted down.

"As Philippe and Patrick would discover on that opening night in Zurich, not everybody would share their enthusiasm or believe in this vision."

There was a shuffle of feet and a ripple of surprise and disbelief.

In hindsight, this was understandable. Imagine going to a cocktail party hosted by the local car dealership and hearing they were going to start manufacturing their own cars. It would not seem realistic. The same dynamic was in play here. Traditionally, only banks issued structured products; they had the expertise, the balance sheets, and the necessary licenses. How could a local broker hope to compete?

That was where GenTwo entered the picture. The host was about to announce—and Patrick and Philippe were about to confirm—that his company was not taking this step alone. It had outsourced the issuance part to GenTwo. Patrick and Philippe were about to tell the crowd that not only was it legally, financially, technically, and organizationally possible to do all this without a bank, but they were already set up and ready to go.

Many of their peers were supportive or at least polite enough to wish them well, but others were dismissive and even hostile. In some cases, the reactions were quite aggressive. One audience member shattered a wine glass on the floor and stomped out, vowing never to speak to Patrick and Philippe again. Later, they received several angry phone calls. It was not a pleasant experience.

Whether angry, incredulous, or jealous, the tone of the pushback was always the same: This will never work. Who do you think you are? Why would anyone choose your unknown fintech startup over the established players and traditional methods? Patrick and Philippe were confident they had the answers, but the only way to prove it was to do it.

DISCOVERING ASSETIZATION

As it turned out, what seemed radical and unsettling that night in Zurich has become quite common today. We've seen that in the steady growth of our platform—client numbers, geographic reach, assets under service, and the variety of products we've helped create have all expanded well beyond what we initially expected. But we also see it in the explosive growth of similar platforms and approaches across the industry. Other firms were reaching the same conclusions, building similar tools, and finding the same demand. We were part of a broader shift.

It was Patrick's cousin Steven Loepfe, who had joined as head of marketing, who gave it the name *assetization*. The word is a portmanteau of "asset" and "democratization" and it captured what we were seeing at the time: the use of securitization to turn almost anything of value into a bankable, investible financial product.

Assetization became the catalyst for the first edition of the book you are reading. That initial book, which was self-published, was released in early 2024 and has since gone through three printings. That edition focused mainly on one aspect of assetization: using securitization tools to make so-called "non-bankable" assets bankable and accessible to investors.

"This showed that something larger was happening than simply ironing out frictions in the securitization process."

Since then, much has changed. Through our work and what we have seen across the industry, it has become clear that assetization is far broader than we first described, and that the real story is the transformation of the investment industry through the democratization of access to assets and the tools of financial product creation. That is why we have written this second, fully reworked edition: to map assetization in its wider sense and to set out where we believe this new infrastructure is heading. We see this in terms of three distinct but overlapping waves:

- **Wave 1: The Democratization of Access.** Wave 1 marks the investment industry's shift from a seller's to a buyer's market, driven by the democratization of access to a wider range of assets. Previously, a handful of large institutions controlled the menu of available investment products, but this is changing as new platforms and tools open up private markets and other alternatives to a broader audience. This "streaming moment" for finance empowers investors to use new building blocks, from private equity funds to thematic ETFs, to curate their own portfolios rather than simply selecting from a pre-approved list. While this wave gives investors significantly more choice and control over their allocations, it has a critical limit: investors can access more, but they still depend on institutions to create the products.
- **Wave 2: The Containerization of Finance.** The second wave disrupts the industry's infrastructure to democratize the creation of financial products, a change comparable to how containerization transformed global trade by standardizing shipping. The complex machinery of product creation—structuring, issuance, and compliance—is being broken down into modular, digital services. This allows financial professionals to wrap any asset or strategy into a standardized "container," such as a security or a token, making the process faster and more cost-effective. By turning product creation into a series of accessible building blocks, this wave moves the capability out of large institutional factories and into the hands of a wider range of users, enabling advisors and wealth managers to shift

from being mere curators to becoming creators of bespoke investment solutions.

- **Wave 3: Radical Automation.** The third wave is the complete automation of the financial product lifecycle, enabling a "prompt to product" world where investment ideas can be transformed into live products in minutes. In this future, AI agents will orchestrate the entire value chain—from structuring and legal documentation to issuance and marketing—based on simple descriptive inputs. This will lead to the rise of open, digital marketplaces where these newly created products can be distributed and discovered, ultimately obliterating the distinction between the buy-side and the sell-side. As the barriers to creation fall, the ability to issue a financial product becomes accessible not just to financial professionals but to any entity with a verifiable asset or cash flow, expanding the investible universe to include almost anything of value.

In the chapters that follow, we unpack these shifts.

The investment industry is transforming

Patrick and Philippe founded GenTwo to solve a specific problem: the friction in traditional securitization. But they quickly realized their work was part of a much larger industry-wide shift. They call this "assetization", a movement that is fundamentally reshaping how financial products get made and who gets to make them.

Chapter Summary

- Patrick and Philippe launched GenTwo in a Zurich nightclub to a skeptical crowd who told them "it will never work."
- Their initial goal was simple: remove friction from traditional securitization, which was too slow, expensive, and exclusive.
- By rethinking infrastructure, they found a way to democratize financial product creation for non-banks.
- They soon realized they weren't alone; a broader wave of innovators was already democratizing the entire value chain.
- This wasn't just a technical fix for one company, but a structural change to the industry's infrastructure.
- They call this collective movement assetization: democratizing both access to assets and the tools to create them.
- It is unfolding in three waves: Access (Wave 1), Creation (Wave 2), and Radical Automation (Wave 3).

"Assetization, powered by technological advancements and tokenization, is unlocking trillions in dormant value — not just expanding the global investment landscape, but redefining what we consider investible in the first place."

Dr. Martha Boeckenfeld, Board Member, Generali Switzerland; Keynote Speaker & Executive Educator, Human-Centric AI

"Assetization is actually democratization. Finally, ordinary investors can access the same opportunities as the privileged few in the oak-paneled boardrooms of Wall Street and The City. The revolution has begun."

Damian Horner, Co-Founder of Vision Creative Labs and Real Vision

CHAPTER TWO

THE BUY SIDE AND ITS DISCONTENTS

I n this chapter we take a look at some of the main drivers of assetization from the perspective of its beneficiaries: investors and the advisors and wealth managers who serve them. Before deep diving into this, however, we'd like you to meet some friends of ours.

MEET ADA, BARBARA, AND CLARK

Ada

From childhood, Ada was immersed in the rhythms of the family business. While other kids played with toys, she was more likely to be found in the workshop, fascinated by the sparkle of stones and the precision of the artisans. She learned the language of the trade as naturally as her mother tongue: how to tell the provenance of gemstones, how to flatter vain clients, and talk intelligently to the clever ones. Summers were spent shadowing her parents, not just for show but for real tasks—welcoming clients at the family's flagship store on Zurich's Bahnhofstrasse, helping in marketing campaigns, or trailing along on business trips. By the time she was a teenager, she knew employees by name, understood how the supply chain worked, and could carry herself in front of demanding clients. Unlike many heirs, she was never forced into the business. She loved it, and everyone could see that she did.

At school, Ada was disciplined and bright. Teachers described her as driven, but also unusually pragmatic for her age. She excelled in languages and business-related subjects, often tying school projects back to the family firm. During secondary school, she began helping with international trade fairs, and it was there she first got a taste of business development: the art of spotting opportunities, making connections, and opening doors.

University widened her horizons. She studied business and culture, mixing economics with courses in history and design. She wanted a broad view of the world into which her family brand sold. While her peers were busy with student clubs or parties, Ada often combined both—running a small event series that was both a social hit and a profitable venture. By her early twenties, she already had a reputation among friends as someone who could *make things work.*

After finishing her MBA at a top European business school, she returned to the family business full-time and quickly advanced to a senior business development position. There, she had responsibility for cultivating new markets and building relationships with younger clients. Her instincts served her well: she was attuned to her generation's demand for transparency, digital-first interactions, and social media marketing.

Ada had always been an avid investor, having started with a little portfolio of penny stocks as a kind of game with her father. By her mid-20s, she had grown this into a tidy little sum of her own. She kept her investment "sandbox" to herself, seeing it as her place to try out new things and take calculated risks: crypto, meme stocks, ESG investing (mostly to find out if it was true, as proponents claimed, that she could "do well by doing good"; it often was). Her private portfolio also let her dabble in whatever investment theme (or fad, she would sometimes smile to herself) being hawked by the finfluencer of the hour. Regardless of whether the investments panned out, this always proved instructive to her.

On her 30th birthday, she received, as per the family charter, her seat on the company board. She also joined the family's semi-formal investment committee, which was run via their private family office. She had a drawerful of new ideas to bring into the committee but knew it would be a challenge. Clark, the family advisor, had her parents' ear. She had known him since she was a child. He was like an uncle to her. She liked him, but they were not on the same wavelength. There was that woman she'd met at the conference—what was her name? She had actually given her her card, which was quaint. Where was it? Ah, there. Barbara. Ada reaches for her laptop.

Barbara

Barbara grew up far from the rarefied world of private banking. Her family background was modest: her parents were practical, hardworking people who valued education but had no connections to finance. Barbara was bright and curious, with a streak of independence. She excelled at school, particularly in math and languages, and was one of those students who seemed equally at ease with numbers and with people. What set her apart early on was her ability to listen—to classmates, to teachers, to anyone.

She was the person friends confided in, a quality that would later become her edge as an advisor.

After secondary school, Barbara landed a junior role at a large private bank. She wasn't hired for pedigree—she entered through one of the institution's apprenticeship programs. At first, she felt out of place: many of her peers were from wealthy families with insider networks. But Barbara made up for it with determination and people skills. Senior colleagues saw her promise, and the bank sponsored her to study finance part-time while continuing her day job. For several years, her life was relentless: long days at the bank, then evenings and weekends in lecture halls. But she persevered, earning her degree and, with it, the credibility to move into advisory work.

She rose steadily, managing increasingly significant accounts, but found herself glancing over the cubicle wall, wishing for more time with her clients and fewer hours decoding compliance checklists. At review meetings, Barbara lingered on the small talk—the new grandchild, the worry about a parent's care—long after the spreadsheets were closed, sensing that these moments mattered just as much as the numbers. But the bank's constraints left her feeling hemmed in, blocked.

By her early 30s, she felt confident that she could do it better on her own. She had gained experience without losing her idealism. With a colleague, she left the bank and set up a boutique advisory practice. The early years were tough. Without the halo of a big brand, winning mandates was a slog. Her first real breakthrough came when an entrepreneurial family, frustrated with their private bank, entrusted her with a slice of their wealth. That became her niche: entrepreneurial families, often spanning generations, who wanted a trusted advisor who could understand both the parents' caution and the children's impatience.

She was a natural in that niche, and by 40, Barbara had a successful boutique with a stable of loyal clients. Or so she hoped. Sitting on Sunday afternoons in her winter garden, she is less and less sure. Doing it better on her own was proving harder than she imagined. She still liked to think she made a difference in her clients' lives. But when she was honest with herself, she wondered if what she had to offer was really still fit for purpose. Or, for that matter, any different than what her peers were offering. She puts down her lavender tea, fires up her browser, and visits her own homepage. She scans the value proposition. And sighs.

Clark

Clark was born into a family of bankers. His father and grandfather had both worked in finance, and it was always assumed he would follow in their footsteps. He had the pedigree: excellent schools, then a top economics degree, followed by a master's at a world-class university. All the ingredients were there for him to become the archetype of the polished, professional banker.

Yet there was always another side to him. Clark had a passion for literature. He read widely—novels, essays, poetry—and wrote short stories in his spare time. He loved the way writers captured human character and frailty. It gave him a sensitivity that would later shape his approach to clients, even if he never pursued writing professionally.

At the private bank where he worked, his career was steady and conventional. He wasn't a showman or a deal-hunter, but he was noticed early by one of the firm's most senior advisors, a man with a legendary client book. Clark became his protégé, learning the craft of wealth management by sitting in on meetings, traveling with him, and observing how trust was built over the course of decades. Through this apprenticeship, he came to know many important families well before he was formally their advisor. When his mentor retired, the portfolio—including Ada's family—passed naturally into Clark's hands.

By 50, Clark was at the height of his career. He had dozens of mandates, a reputation for reliability, and the quiet respect of his colleagues. But he also remained decidedly, even doggedly, old school. He remembered details that others forgot: a throwaway comment made years before, the name of a grandchild, a personal worry expressed in passing. Clients trusted him not only with their assets but also with their doubts and family tensions.

The paradox about Clark was that, while he was old-school as a banker, outside the office, he was not. He kept up with the world around him. He read contemporary fiction, went to author readings, and frequented gallery openings. And not for show: he liked keeping up with whatever was buzzing in the culture—fintech, crypto, longevity, sustainability. And, of course, all this helped him understand where his clients and their children were coming from.

Or so he liked to think. The truth was, like Barbara, he was increasingly unsure. What he saw and heard convinced him that continuity—the bedrock of his career—was under pressure. While he was still bringing in new assets, his outflows were increasing. It was often the younger ones pulling the trigger. The thing was, he actually understood them. But he couldn't convince them that he did. The irony of his position was that even if he could convince them, he didn't have much to offer, certainly not what they were looking for. An email from Ada arrives with the agenda for the next family investment committee meeting. He decides to open it later.

THE ZEITGEIST
OF ASSETIZATION

Ada, Barbara, and Clark are of course not real people. They are personas we first introduced in the original edition of our book to represent the main protagonists of assetization. As representatives of the zeitgeist of assetization, they continue to reflect a wider mood in the investment world–a sense that the system no longer matches what its users want it to do.

Ada reflects today's investor—a person shaped by her exposure to both long-standing family business traditions and the hyper-connected, digital world. We deliberately made her young because it is the younger generation driving most of these changes: Millennials, Gen Z, and other groups set to inherit significant wealth and redefine investing in their own way. But it's not just the young. Across all generations, investors are questioning why the industry's default products and processes still resemble those used by their parents or grandparents. Ada stands for those who are no longer willing to wait for permission or be told to "trust the system"; she seeks immediacy, genuine agency, and access to opportunities that mirror her reality and values.

"Ada, Barbara, and Clark represent the zeitgeist of assetization, the environment in which today's investment story unfolds."

Barbara represents the independent advisor—professionals who have built their value on close, personal client relationships and a hands-on approach to achieving bespoke outcomes. She represents boutiques, family offices, and entrepreneurial wealth managers who balance world-class service with limited resources. Barbara's biggest concern is staying relevant in a crowded market where technology and large institutions make it harder to stand out. She wants to deliver truly personal, differentiated advice, but faces relentless pressure from standardization, compliance burdens, and commoditized products that threaten to blur her value proposition. She worries about maintaining her edge, continuing to make a real difference for clients, and adapting fast enough in a landscape where yesterday's strengths risk becoming today's liabilities.

Clark represents the institutional wealth managers of the world, operating within private banks and the wealth management divisions of large universal banks. His career is grounded in tradition, reputation, and long-standing client relationships. But Clark feels the ground shifting beneath him. He faces growing pressure to adapt to new client demands—faster execution, new asset classes, and technology-driven service—without losing what made his approach valuable in the first place. He worries that relying solely on legacy and trust may no longer be enough for a new generation of clients, who expect speed, transparency, and innovation. Clark is constantly balancing a deep respect for tradition with the need to reinvent, uncertain how to honor the past while ensuring he and his institution remain relevant. Like many of his peers, he knows that failing to evolve risks obsolescence, yet changing too quickly could mean losing the very strengths that built his reputation.

What unites Ada, Barbara, and Clark is the fact that they are all "consumers" of investment products. Ada does so directly. Barbara and Clark are indirect consumers, as a significant part of their job involves advising their clients on what to buy. In the jargon, they are referred to as "allocators" because they are helping with asset allocation decisions. We group them together under the term "buy side."[1] The important distinction is that they generally do not get involved in creating financial products. That's the provenance of the large institutional asset managers—the "sell side" that determines the available product shelf.

In our opinion, dissatisfaction with the investment industry status quo among investors and their advisors is one of the main—if not the main— drivers of assetization. While this dissatisfaction is expressed in a wide range of areas, there are certain trends that stand out from an assetization perspective.

PUBLIC MARKETS ARE SHRINKING

One major problem is that public markets are no longer representative of the full economy.

When most people think of investing, they think of the familiar world of public markets: stocks, bonds, mutual funds, and ETFs—all the standard financial instruments that you can buy and sell, instantaneously, on public exchanges. Whether through a pension plan, brokerage account, or an app, nearly everyone's wealth is funneled into this vast system.

And vast is the appropriate word: public markets are immense. Trillions of dollars flow through them daily. Global stocks are worth around $125 trillion, and bonds are nearly $145 trillion.[2] Public markets infrastructure is extremely advanced: exchanges open, prices shift, portfolios rebalance like magic, all behind a user-friendly digital façade. Most investors see only the clean pie charts, never the complex machinery of custody chains, regulations, and risk management that keep it all running.

That's the good news. The bad news is that public markets are far more limited in scope than they appear. We're not talking about market cap, but about asset diversity. In America, the number of listed firms has halved over three decades, from nearly 8,000 in the late 1990s to fewer than 4,300 today.[3] The ones that are left are getting bloated: the ten largest stocks now make up almost 40% of the S&P 500's value.[4]

"One major problem is that public markets are no longer representative of the full economy."

There are several reasons for this.

Being public has become expensive and complex. New rules introduced after the corporate scandals and financial crises of the 2000s—Sarbanes-Oxley in the United States and MiFID in Europe—made markets safer but also increased the bureaucratic burden. Compliance, disclosure, ESG reports, constant audits: a mid-sized company might spend over a million dollars a year just on paperwork. Add to that the distraction of quarterly earnings calls and activist shareholders, and many executives now see staying private as the more sensible option. It's far easier to pursue long-term goals without the relentless glare of the next quarter's stock price.

Meanwhile, the public companies that remain continue to swallow up the competition. For every new IPO, five or six mergers or acquisitions quietly shrink the list. The market is becoming tall and thin—a handful of dominant giants at the top. Apple and Microsoft alone are worth nearly one in every seven dollars in the S&P 500. The so-called "Magnificent 7" tech firms drive most of the index's returns.

This growing concentration means public markets no longer represent the full sweep of economic activity. The S&P 500, for instance, accounts for roughly a fifth of American jobs and half of corporate profits, but its share of GDP is shrinking. As one JPMorgan researcher put it, today "markets are not the economy."[5] Many sectors, including private companies, infrastructure, private credit, and emerging asset classes, are either underrepresented or missing entirely.

Innovation and growth are happening elsewhere: some 80% of American firms with revenues above $100 million remain private. And it's not just the US. Percentages are even higher in the European Union and the United Kingdom.[6] In the meantime, the number of private-equity-backed companies has soared. That means that value creation increasingly happens off-exchange, unseen and unowned by the typical saver. By the time a business finally goes public, the biggest gains have often already been captured by private funders. For the average investor, the opportunity set is shrinking at the same time that the real economy is becoming more diverse.

PUBLIC MARKETS ARE BECOMING MORE CORRELATED

Another problem is that public markets are becoming more correlated, reducing the diversification effect.

Classic portfolio theory, dating back to Harry Markowitz in the 1950s, promised that diversifying across stocks and bonds would cushion shocks. This approach—eventually codified in the "60/40 portfolio" (60% stocks, 40% bonds)—became the industry standard for decades. The logic was straightforward: when stocks fell, bonds typically rose, and vice versa. For years, this "free lunch" of diversification held up.

But no longer. Today, markets tend to move in lockstep more often. Several factors are at play: the rise of index funds and passive investing means huge flows move entire markets together; algorithmic trading amplifies reactions to global news; and economic shocks now ripple instantly across borders. The result is that, in several recent episodes, stocks and bonds have fallen in tandem. International investing, once a reliable way to spread risk, offers little refuge—correlations between assets and across regions are higher than ever. This appears to be a permanent shift, not just a temporary trend. According to a BlackRock research note: "At the heart of asset allocation decisions lies the textbook relationship that stocks and bonds have had a negative correlation: when stocks go down as company prospects deteriorate, investors may turn to bonds in search of safer assets. This has remained the core underpinning of many portfolios' most basic asset allocation breakdown. . . .But we believe this relationship has fundamentally shifted; less reliable correlations undermine the diversification benefits the two core asset classes provided each other."[7]

The "free lunch" of diversification is disappearing, at least in public markets. Portfolios built solely from public equities and bonds are both less diverse and more exposed to systemic shocks.

It's little wonder, then, that investors are increasingly dissatisfied and on the hunt for alternatives. The gaps in the old system are growing wider, and the search for new sources of growth—and genuine diversification—has become urgent.

INVESTORS ARE POURING MONEY INTO PRIVATE MARKETS

As a result, investors are looking for alternative investments outside the public markets—for instance, in what are known as private markets.

These markets—private equity, private credit, infrastructure, and real estate—differ from public markets in one key respect: they are not listed. Investors buy into companies, loans, and physical assets directly, off-the-grid of public exchanges.

"It's little wonder, then, that investors are increasingly dissatisfied and on the hunt for alternatives."

These markets have grown rapidly in recent years. Assets under management stood at $10 trillion in 2021 and are projected to reach $18 trillion by 2027.[8]

Such growth is only possible because investor demand is surging.

Institutions have led the way. Pension funds, insurers, and other large investors have steadily increased allocations to private markets—now often dedicating up to a third of their portfolios to these assets.

Private investors are following. Advisors now routinely include alternatives like private equity and real estate in client portfolios—and expect to do more in the future.

Accredited investors held an estimated $2–2.5 trillion in private capital in 2025, while retail investors accounted for about $1 trillion. Forecasts suggest US retail investors will approach $2.5 trillion in private markets by 2030, with Europeans reaching $3.3 trillion.[9]

In short, private markets have gone from a niche option to a must-have for investors looking to expand their opportunities and protect their portfolios from the ups and downs of traditional financial markets.

INVESTORS ARE INCREASINGLY INTERESTED IN NEW OR EXOTIC ASSET CLASSES

The search for alternatives is also driving investors into new asset classes. One of the most prominent is cryptocurrencies.

In the past two years, crypto has gone from fringe asset to mainstream destination for both individual and institutional capital. The turning point came when the U.S. approved Bitcoin and Ethereum spot ETFs in early 2024. These regulated vehicles gave investors—especially large institutions—a secure, familiar way to access crypto, and the response was immediate. As we were writing this book, investment flows were surging, with new ETFs shattering records for speed and scale. BlackRock's Bitcoin ETF quickly became its fastest-growing fund ever, with money pouring in from both retail and institutional investors.[10]

It's not just Bitcoin. Ethereum ETFs have also drawn strong inflows, as investors seek broader crypto exposure.

But it does not stop with digital assets. We are also seeing increased interest in what are sometimes called "passion" assets, like art and collectibles.

What is the benefit? One advantage is that art and collectibles usually do not fluctuate in value at the same time as the stock market. This means they can help "diversify" an investor's portfolio—if stocks decline, a valuable painting or a rare bottle of wine might hold steady or even increase in value. Art prices also tend to remain strong because more and more wealthy individuals are willing to buy famous works, while the number of truly great masterpieces stays limited. Additionally, the art market is global. If a seller can't find a buyer in one part of the world, there's a good chance someone elsewhere will be interested.

It's not just the super-rich getting involved anymore. New platforms let people buy small shares of valuable artworks, so you can own a fraction of a famous painting for as little as $1,000. This type of "fractional" investing in art has grown rapidly over the past few years and is expected to continue expanding. More and more people are joining in.

INVESTORS ARE DISSATISFIED WITH THE STATUS QUO

Along with a lack of choice in public markets driving investors to look for alternative opportunities, we think a deep-seated dissatisfaction with the status quo of the investment industry more generally is a major driver of assetization.

This is hardly a radical claim. Shifting investor demand—particularly among younger clients—is now one of the hottest topics in wealth management, as countless industry surveys and reports make clear.[11] Several themes stand out from an assetization perspective.

Trust in financial advisors and big investment firms is declining. Many people no longer automatically believe these institutions act in their best interests. They question whether an advisor truly understands their situation, communicates clearly, or offers value that justifies the fees. When individuals inherit wealth or face major financial decisions, they more frequently seek new advisors or platforms rather than sticking with their family's usual advisor out of habit. Although performance and fees are still important, unfulfilled needs and poor communication often motivate people to switch. As

"There is a deep-seated dissatisfaction with the status quo of the investment industry."

trust diminishes, loyalty shifts from firms to individual advisors—if those advisors meet expectations. Even with declining general trust, loyalty to a single trusted advisor can remain very strong when clients feel genuinely understood.

Demand for digital tools is also growing. Investors increasingly expect to access their finances through apps and websites, getting answers and completing transactions instantly. The old routine—waiting for a meeting in a banker's office—no longer matches the speed of modern investing. Whether they are checking balances, adjusting portfolios, or seeking advice, investors want intuitive platforms that work anytime. Firms that provide fast, seamless digital experiences tend to keep their clients; those that cling to slow, clunky processes quickly lose them.

More and more investors want the ability to design their own portfolios. They want to research options, compare platforms, and act independently without having to rely on advisors. Digital tools—from automated analytics to mobile apps—increasingly give them that control while still offering guidance. They haven't abandoned expert advice; they simply want to decide when and how to use it. What matters is agency: the ability to chart a financial course on their own, with help available only when they choose to seek it.

Perhaps not surprisingly, the most profound shifts in investor behavior are happening among the young.

For many younger investors, values matter just as much as returns. Portfolios increasingly reflect personal beliefs about social impact, environmental issues, or technological innovation. The line between "traditional" and "alternative" investing is fading as sustainable strategies, crypto, thematic funds, and private markets become mainstream. People want their money to help shape the future, not just sit quietly in a fund.

That said, while enthusiasm for sustainable and impact-focused investing remains strong, many younger investors hold volatile assets—especially cryptocurrencies. At the same time, there is a clear appetite for high-risk, high-reward opportunities. Taking risks has become more accepted. They feel more comfortable exploring digital assets or other unconventional options, perhaps because the future seems less certain and traditional methods often feel too slow. In uncertain times, bold bets can seem like a logical way to stay ahead.

Social channels now shape financial decisions alongside professional advice. Viral trends, online communities, and "finfluencers" on TikTok or Instagram steer where money flows. Social media delivers not just information but also relatability and emotional momentum, which can spur quick decisions or rapid shifts in direction.

ADVISORS AND WEALTH MANAGERS ARE UNDER PRESSURE

Financial advisors everywhere are feeling the same pressures as their clients. They see the growing interest in alternative assets, the stronger focus on sustainability, and the impatience with traditional products. With client preferences changing rapidly—driven by social media trends, market FOMO, and a wish for more control—the old strategies just aren't cutting it anymore.

Independent advisors and boutiques often face big hurdles when it comes to operations. They might not have the size, infrastructure, or licensing needed to respond swiftly to client requests for private markets, thematic products, or customized solutions. Innovation can feel slow and expensive, often depending on third-party platforms or the slower processes of larger institutions. By the time a new product or strategy gets approved, clients' interests might have already shifted elsewhere.

Institutional advisors encounter their own unique challenges. Their product options are frequently guided more by committee decisions and company priorities than by what clients actually want. Recommendations are typically limited to what the institution makes or white-labels, which means advisors sometimes watch as younger clients move their assets elsewhere to pursue opportunities that the institution can't provide. Even when institutions push for innovation, those on the front lines often have little say in what gets developed, leaving them to manage the fallout when clients chase trends or take risks beyond the advisor's control.

> *"The many pressures faced by advisors and wealth managers originate from a fundamental tension: they are consumers, not creators, of the products they recommend."*

The old-school wealth management approach—diversified portfolios with blue-chip stocks and a few alternatives—no longer fully resonates with today's clients. They're now looking for access to late-stage startups, private credit, tokenized assets, and impactful investments. Clients also expect quicker execution, lower minimum investments, more transparency, and importantly, the freedom to experiment with parts of their portfolios. Advisors have the rewarding yet challenging duty of guiding this exploration while protecting clients from potential mistakes—a delicate balance that's not always easy to achieve.

These challenges are just some of the issues the industry faces—we will explore them further in Chapter 6. What's truly interesting is that many pressures faced by advisors and wealth managers originate from a fundamental tension: advisors are often consumers, not creators, of the products they recommend. Their flexibility is somewhat limited by the priorities of large asset managers, who are compelled to focus on size rather than offering personalized, modular solutions. Advisors genuinely want to be architects of solutions, not just middlemen selling off-the-shelf products. They aim to provide both expert guidance and independence to their clients—balancing careful discipline with innovative thinking. However, until the system evolves, many find themselves caught between traditional models and the changing needs of their clients.

THE BUY SIDE IS DRIVING CHANGE

This chapter highlights how the investment industry is evolving, with much of this change starting on the buy side—the Adas, Barbaras, and Clarks of the world. Their frustrations and aspirations are powerful forces driving the system toward new ways of access, products, and advice. The personas we introduced help us keep this dynamic in view. They allow us to see how these pressures appear in various lives and how, collectively, they challenge the current limits of our infrastructure.

Of course, the buy side is not acting alone. Technology, regulation, and macroeconomic shifts all make change possible. But without this persistent demand from investors and their advisors, little would move. In the chapters that follow, we look at how the industry is transforming—first by expanding access (Wave 1), then by reengineering the machinery of the financial product creation value chain itself (Wave 2), and finally by introducing radical automation and scaling (Wave 3).

NOTES

1. This is a slightly idiosyncratic use of the term, as "buy side" usually refers to the institutional investors.
2. SIFMA (2025). *2025 Capital Markets Fact Book*. https://www.sifma.org/wp-content/uploads/2024/07/2025-SIFMA-Capital-Markets-Factbook.pdf (accessed 28 November 2025).

3. JPMorgan Chase & Co. (2024). *Jamie Dimon's Letter to Shareholders, Annual Report 2023.* https://www.jpmorganchase.com/ir/annual-report/2023/ar-ceo-letters (accessed 28 November 2025).

4. Foelber, D. "*The 'Ten Titans' Stocks Now Make Up 38% of the S&P 500*," Nasdaq, August 24, 2025, https://www.nasdaq.com/articles/ten-titans-stocks-now-make-38-sp-500-heres-what-it-means-your-investment-portfolio.

5. J.P. Morgan Private Bank (2025). *Why the U.S. Economy and S&P 500 Are Diverging.* https://privatebank.jpmorgan.com/apac/en/insights/markets-and-investing/tmt/why-the-us-economy-and-sp-500-are-diverging (accessed 28 November 2025).

6. Fink, L. (2025). *Larry Fink's 2025 Chairman's Letter to Investors.* https://www.blackrock.com/corporate/investor-relations/larry-fink-annual-chairmans-letter (accessed 28 November 2025).

7. BlackRock (2025). *2025 Fall Investment Directions: Rethinking Diversification.* https://www.blackrock.com/us/financial-professionals/insights/investment-directions-fall-2025 (accessed 28 November 2025).

8. S&P Global (2025). *Private Markets – A Growing, Alternative Asset Class.* https://www.spglobal.com/en/research-insights/market-insights/private-markets (accessed 28 November 2025).

9. Deloitte (2025). *Increasing Retail Client Exposure to Private Capital Investing.* https://www.deloitte.com/us/en/insights/industry/financial-services/financial-services-industry-predictions/2025/private-capital-investing.html (accessed 28 November 2025).

10. Fortune (2025). *BlackRock's Most Profitable ETF Is a Nearly $100 Billion Bitcoin Giant.* https://fortune.com/crypto/2025/10/07/blackrock-etf-ibit-bitcoin-most-profitable-crypto/ (accessed 28 November 2025).

11. See: McKinsey & Company (2025). *Asset Management 2025: The Great Convergence.* https://www.mckinsey.com/industries/financial-services/our-insights/asset-management-2025-the-great-convergence (accessed 28 November 2025); World Economic Forum (2024). *The Future of Financial Advice.* https://www3.weforum.org/docs/WEF_The_Future_of_Financial_Advice_2024.pdf (accessed 28 November 2025); EY (2025). *2025 EY Global Wealth Research Report.* https://fundhub.co.za/wp-content/uploads/sites/2/2025/07/ey-2025-global-wealth-research-report.pdf (accessed 28 November 2025).

The buy side is demanding change

Investors, independent advisors, and institutional wealth managers are all currently trapped in a "consumer" role—forced to choose from a limited shelf of products created by large institutions. This status quo is no longer working. Shrinking public markets and generic products are failing to meet the needs of a modern, digital-first generation.

Chapter Summary

- The investment world is split into two camps: the "buy side" (investors/advisors) and the "sell side" (banks/issuers).
- Currently, the buy side is trapped in a consumer role, forced to accept whatever the sell side creates.
- This status quo is failing: public markets are shrinking, with the number of listed firms halving in three decades.
- Rising correlations between stocks and bonds have broken traditional safety models like the 60/40 portfolio.
- Investors are urgently seeking "real" diversification in private equity, credit, and digital assets.
- Meanwhile, a digital-first generation demands transparency, agency, and values-aligned portfolios.
- Advisors feel the squeeze: they face fee compression and commoditization from robo-platforms.
- To survive and thrive, the buy side needs tools to stop just consuming products and start creating them.

"Assetization is one of the most important developments in the quest to democratize access to investment opportunities. It helps foster prosperity for all."

Dr. Steffen Pauls, Founder and CEO of Moonfare; Former Managing Director and Head of Germany at KKR

"Assetization expands what investors can reach—and that expansion creates the conditions for the next generation of financial innovation."

Nathaniel T. Bradley, CEO, Datavault AI

CHAPTER THREE

WAVE 1—THE DEMOCRATIZATION OF ACCESS

I n this chapter we make the case that, while finance has always been a seller's market where institutions decided what products should exist, we're now witnessing a fundamental transition to a buyer's market where investors have much more choice to decide what they should own. If you are an investor, this is of course good news, but there's a caveat: control of financial product creation remains in the hands of a relatively few industry giants. Your choices are still ultimately limited.

THE INVESTMENT INDUSTRY USED TO BE A SELLER'S MARKET

The story of modern finance is one of steady expansion. From the Dutch East India Company's public shares in the 1600s, through investment trusts in the 1800s, to mutual funds and online brokerages in the 1900s, each wave brought more products and more access to more people. By the early 21st century, the industry had reached remarkable scale: tens of thousands of funds, global exchanges, and digital platforms offering instant access to markets worldwide.

Yet despite this expansion, one fundamental thing hasn't changed.

Look behind the shiny screens of investment platforms around the world, and you'll find that control of production is firmly in the hands of a relatively small number of powerful institutions: global banks, asset managers, mutual fund companies, ETF sponsors, and broker-dealer networks. These organizations act as the architects and gatekeepers of the entire investment menu.

Virtually every product available to investors—whether a broad-market index fund, an emerging market ETF, or a thematic basket—has been designed, constructed, and brought to market by these large financial institutions. Fund lineups, strategies, and features are determined within corporate boardrooms and product committees, based on what these firms believe is profitable, scalable, and marketable. Of course this includes taking into account what investors want. But that's not the only factor, and it presupposes that product designers actually understand their clients' needs.

"Until the turn of the millennium, the investment industry resembled the music industry before streaming."

Once created, products are heavily marketed via distribution channels controlled by the same organizations—investment platforms, supermarket-style fund lists, broker recommendations, and model portfolios.

This centralization goes beyond product design. Fees, minimum investments, rebalancing schedules, and operational structures are all set by the product creators. Even with online platforms, most investors see only the products curated by these gatekeepers—highlighted by lists, ratings, and promotional campaigns. New funds or strategies are subject to approval and sponsorship by large institutions; "off-the-shelf" really means "from the factory floor of a handful of giants."

There are good reasons for this.

Building investment products takes specialist expertise. It also costs money, and not just for the expertise. Laws governing investments—especially mutual funds and investment companies—set strict rules around disclosure, risk management, and investor protection. These rules favor large organizations that can absorb compliance costs and navigate regulatory complexity.

It's really only the large institutions that have the necessary economies of scale. For these reasons investing has been, for most of its history, an industry where large sellers control the menu.

INVESTING IS NOW BECOMING A BUYER'S MARKET

At least, that was the case through the end of the 20th century. We'd argue that, around the turn of the millennium, the traditional investment industry looked a lot like the music industry just before streaming: dominated by powerful gatekeepers, with investors forced to choose from a narrow, pre-set menu.

Before Spotify and Apple Music, music was mostly in the hands of record labels, studios, and music distributors. These gatekeepers decided which songs would reach listeners, how albums were put together, and which genres got the spotlight. Music was mainly distributed physically— through CDs, tapes, and vinyl—available only through carefully chosen channels. Listeners could only pick from what was available on store shelves. Even if there was a strong interest in niche genres or new artists, supply was limited to what the labels thought would be profitable or strategically important. Essentially, consumers played a reactive role: they could choose from a catalogue but had little influence over what was offered next or how they discovered new music.

Streaming changed everything. Suddenly, listeners weren't bound to the catalogues curated by record labels, nor did they have to buy physical albums or even digital downloads. Today you can choose from almost unlimited, on-demand access to millions of songs across every imaginable genre and era. Personal playlists, algorithmic recommendations, and near-instant discovery are now the norm. Music fans are no longer passive consumers—they have become active participants, curators, and creators of their own listening experience. It has, to a large extent, been transformed into a buyer's market.

We think something similar is now happening in finance. And we'd point to the rise of the ETF as our exhibit number one.

Since the first US ETF launched in 1993, the industry has exploded. It is difficult to overstate the size. As of October 2025, the global ETF industry encompasses over 15,000 products, representing a record $18.8 trillion in assets under management. The United States alone accounts for nearly $13 trillion in ETF assets, with new launches averaging more than 750 funds per year.[1]

The rise of ETFs has come at the expense of traditional asset managers. In the first nine months of 2025 alone, investors withdrew nearly $500 billion from US mutual funds and invested over $1 trillion in ETFs, setting records.[2] This, in turn, is forcing a wave of closures. Many small active managers are losing relevance and struggling to attract new inflows. As a result, we're seeing an acceleration of fund liquidations and conversions to ETF structures, as managers scramble to adapt to mounting margin pressure.[3]

"ETFs began to turn investing from a seller's into a buyer's market."

THE ETF REVOLUTION IS ABOUT CHOICE, NOT COST

Conventional wisdom attributes this to cost. ETFs charge lower fees than actively managed funds. Performance is often comparable or better. Passive wins because it's cheaper. Simple economics.

But we think that explanation misses what's actually happening.

We believe the ETF boom isn't fundamentally about passive versus active or even about fees. It's about where decision-making happens. In the traditional model, a fund manager picks stocks and you trust their judgment. The manager decides which sectors to overweight, which companies to buy, and when to rebalance. Your role is to select the manager and hope they're right.

With ETFs, that began to flip. Now investors can make their own allocation decisions. They can choose between sector ETFs, thematic ETFs, factor ETFs, international ETFs, fixed income ETFs. Thousands of building blocks, each tracking a specific slice of the market. That allows investors to decide which sectors to emphasize, which themes to pursue, which factors matter. The individual funds may be passive, but the investor isn't. The investor can make active portfolio construction decisions at the user level.

This is what a buyer's market means in finance. Not lower prices or oversupply in the traditional economic sense, but control. In a seller's market, institutions decide what you should own. In a buyer's market, you decide.

BlackRock and Vanguard are crushing everyone, not because they're passive per se or because of their fees per se, but because they've built infrastructure that serves the buyer's market. They understood that investors want to make their own choices about what to own and how to weight it.

The firms losing market share aren't losing because they're "active"— they're losing because they still operate as if they get to decide what investors should buy. The paradox is striking: the industry appears more concentrated than ever, with a few giants dominating, yet it's simultaneously becoming more individualized, as millions of investors make their own allocation decisions using those giants' tools. The ones who serve the buyer's market are the ones winning.

DEMOCRATIZATION OF ACCESS IS THE FIRST WAVE OF ASSETIZATION

You could say that ETFs were the industry's streaming moment. We also see them as the start of the first wave of assetization. Lately, this wave has been speeding up. We can observe this in three areas:

- **First, the convergence of public and private markets.** The mainstream investment industry is racing to give ordinary investors access to private markets. What used to require multimillion-dollar minimums and insider connections is now being transformed into retail-friendly options. BlackRock, JPMorgan, KKR, and other major players are investing billions in this trend. The motivation is obvious: trillions in untapped demand from investors seeking exposure to private equity, private credit, infrastructure, and real assets but who have been kept out by traditional barriers.

- **Second, new digital platforms are speeding up this democratization.** A wave of fintech entrants is completely bypassing traditional gatekeepers. These platforms provide direct access to alternatives that used to be reserved only for institutions and ultra-high-net-worth individuals. For accredited investors like Ada and advisors like Barbara, the options have grown significantly in just the past few years.
- **Third, DIY finance tools are giving investors direct control over portfolio construction.** Zero-commission trading and fractional shares make it practical to assemble and adjust diversified portfolios one position at a time. Robo-advisors offer an automated starting point, while direct indexing lets investors fine-tune or completely redesign an index to match their own preferences, values, and tax needs. Each of these tools shifts the decisive step of building and maintaining a portfolio from institutions to individual investors. The infrastructure that once demanded significant wealth and professional support now lets anyone with a smartphone and a few thousand dollars construct a portfolio on their own terms if they so desire.

Let's look at them in detail.

PUBLIC AND PRIVATE MARKETS ARE CONVERGING

At the Milken Institute Global Conference 2025, there was a very interesting panel on the merging of public and private markets. It featured representatives from the world's largest asset managers and banks, including

Blackstone, BNY, Goldman, and Citi, as well as new entrants to the space such as CAIS and Motive Partners.

While the panel covered a wide range of topics, there was general agreement on the basic theme: the public and private markets are converging, and this convergence is occurring rapidly. In the not-too-distant future, we can expect almost total democratization of access to private markets—things like private equity, private credit, and other alternatives—in the same way we have seen it happen on public markets with platforms like Robinhood. As one panelist put it, "I remember buying a mutual fund with a subscription document. Now we buy a mutual fund instantly with the push of a button. It's not too far away until every alternative is being purchased that way."[4]

Look again at the companies represented on the Milken Institute panel mentioned above, and it's clear that the mainstream of the investment industry is playing a significant role in the democratization of private markets—either on their own or in partnership with alternative asset managers, technology providers, and others. In our view, this represents a significant bet on assetization.

> *"Soon, every alternative asset will be purchased with the push of a button."*

The incentives are clear: the sheer scale of untapped capital, the shift in economic growth to private companies, and the sense that the private markets represent a "blue ocean" that is far from saturated. As one panelist put it, in the United States alone, there could be "upwards of $10 trillion over the next decade coming out of wealth management and investing in alternative investment strategies."

To tap into that, the industry has had to work to remove the barriers that have traditionally hindered private investors. These are well-known. In the past, if Ada wanted to get into private equity, she would have had to deal with minimum investment requirements that often started at $5 million or even $10 million. If she had the money, it didn't automatically mean she could find a suitable fund: getting to the best opportunities often requires the right connections. Without these connections, Ada would face a daunting task in choosing the right fund. At a Bloomberg event in 2025, Alisa Wood, a partner at KKR, famously pointed out that there are more private equity funds in the United States than there are McDonald's (19,000 to 14,000).[5] That's a lot of data to sift through. And if she does find something she likes, making the investment is nowhere near as easy or straightforward as on her trading platforms: there is a lot of paperwork and overhead to take care of, fund subscription documents, private placement memoranda, AML/KYC forms, and limited partnership agreements. The list goes on. Having navigated all of this to make the investment, Ada would find her money tied up. Typical private equity funds involve lockups of a decade or more. Due to fees and the lag between investing in the fund and the fund deploying the capital, she could actually expect to lose money, at least on paper, during the first few years (this is known as the J-curve in private equity investments).

The good news for Ada is that, thanks to ongoing industry innovations, these barriers have been gradually coming down. This means she has more choices.

For example, she could choose an evergreen fund. These are open-ended private market vehicles that allow investors to enter or exit at periodic intervals, rather than at fixed dates. Unlike traditional private equity funds, which have a set term and draw down capital as needed, evergreen funds raise and deploy capital continuously, offering more liquidity and lower minimum investment requirements. Investors gain immediate exposure, and fund managers reinvest profits into new deals, thereby maintaining a perpetual portfolio. This addresses issues such as long lockups and the J-curve. This is more palatable to many types of investors, although it still falls far short of the daily liquidity of public markets. These funds are also called "semi-liquid" because the rules typically allow investors to withdraw their money only occasionally, usually every three months, and then cap the amount that can be withdrawn at any one time, typically up to 5% of the fund's assets.[6]

Or she could invest in a feeder fund. These funds pool capital from many smaller investors (sometimes through platforms or wealth managers) and invest it in a larger, master private-market fund—a structure often referred to as a "master-feeder." This allows investors to participate in deals and funds that would otherwise require significantly higher minimums, essentially giving small investors a "seat at the table" alongside institutions. Otherwise, however, this is a standard private equity fund investment. Ada will generally need to contend with the associated long lockups and J-curve.

If she's interested in other types of private market assets, she'll find evergreen and feeder fund structures now available not just for private equity, but also for private credit and infrastructure. In private credit, these vehicles let investors pool capital to lend directly to companies at negotiated rates, opening up access to corporate credit that was once the domain of banks and institutions. In infrastructure, evergreen and feeder funds invest in large-scale projects—roads, bridges, renewable energy—providing a steady stream of income linked to project revenues. In each case, these innovations are extending the private markets playbook across new asset classes.

While the instruments we've described so far do open up access to many more types of investors, these are still typically reserved for qualified or accredited investors, who meet certain minimum wealth requirements set by regulators.

Even though Ada qualifies as an accredited investor, she doesn't need to rely solely on specialist platforms or private banks to access private markets. Increasingly, a new generation of products is being designed for the broader retail audience—available right alongside stocks and ETFs on her online brokerage account.

She can try an interval fund, for example. These are structured much like mutual funds: investors can buy in at any time, but withdrawals are only permitted at set intervals—typically quarterly. This feature gives the fund manager the flexibility to invest in less liquid private assets. Interval funds are regulated under the same framework as mutual funds, so their terms are clear and transparent.[7]

Ada also now has access to a growing crop of private market ETFs and so-called hybrid funds, which are built specifically for retail investors. These vehicles package hard-to-access assets—like private equity or private credit—into regulated funds that can be bought and sold on her usual brokerage platform, just like any listed security. Partnerships between major asset managers and alternative specialists are making this possible; for instance, State Street and Apollo have teamed up to launch ETFs that combine public bonds with a significant allocation to directly sourced private credit.[8] Other funds, such as those from BlackRock and Partners Group, blend public and private equity.[9] On the hybrid fund front, global firms like KKR and Capital Group are introducing multi-sector portfolios that allocate a significant portion to private assets, with the rest in public markets—all with low minimums and the convenience of quarterly liquidity.[10] In every case, teams of managers and sponsors handle the sourcing, access, and valuation of private market holdings, while trading and reporting are handled through familiar, regulated structures.

> *"The mainstream of the investment industry is betting on assetization."*

This is the future that the panelists at the Milken Institute event discussed. And it's just the beginning. We can expect more innovation and more convergence between the familiar public markets investment world and the private and alternative markets. The incentives for the industry are just too great.

The main point we are trying to make is not the relative merits of the different types of investments, however. Our point is that the mainstream of the investment industry, the heavy hitters, are betting on assetization. They are the driving forces behind this first wave.

NEW PLATFORMS ARE ACCELERATING THIS DEMOCRATIZATION

It's not just the established players who have responded to the demand for private market access. We're also seeing a surge of innovation from alternative asset managers and a new generation of digital platforms—each aiming to democratize alternatives in their own way.

For Ada, who qualifies as an accredited investor, this means a wealth of new options. Digital platforms like Moonfare are designed specifically for individuals like her, offering direct access to institutional-quality private equity, private credit, and a growing selection of alternative assets. Unlike the old model, where private markets were the exclusive domain of private banks and wealth managers, Ada can now browse, compare, and invest in funds herself. Moonfare, for example, pools investor assets into feeder funds, reducing minimums and increasing choices; onboarding is simple, with a variety of direct, co-investment, and semi-liquid options.

Barbara also enjoys the benefits of this digital transformation wave. Platforms like iCapital and CAIS act as B2B gateways for advisors, providing a modern marketplace where Barbara and her colleagues can easily find, subscribe to, and manage private market investments for their clients. These platforms take care of legal details, operational tasks, and reporting, freeing up Barbara to focus more on helping her clients achieve their goals rather than getting caught up in paperwork. For example, CAIS includes features like secondary market trading and a broader range of assets, all working smoothly together to support wealth managers and advisors.

A bit further from the mainstream—but moving rapidly toward it— are the tokenization platforms. These use blockchain technology to turn rights to real or financial assets into digital tokens. Platforms like Securitize now offer a range of private market investments, including private equity, credit, and crypto, often with lower minimums and new liquidity options. For Ada, this means setting up a digital wallet or exchange account, but the process is getting easier all the time.

Blockchains provide an interesting infrastructure for investors. Digital tokens can be traded 24/7, not just during market hours, and transfers between buyers and sellers happen almost instantly, with settlement times measured in minutes rather than days. Smart contracts automate much of the paperwork and administration, reducing friction and the risk of errors. As shared records of ownership, blockchains can, in theory, add efficiencies by cutting out layers of intermediaries. We will discuss blockchain and tokens in more detail in a later chapter. From Ada's perspective, however, tokenization offers potentially greater flexibility, speed, and control, as well as the potential for lower costs and access to global markets, all from her laptop or phone. This is one reason why companies like BlackRock are racing to tokenize their funds.

The list of new platforms and approaches is extensive and continually expanding. The point isn't to be exhaustive, but to show just how many players—old and new—are betting on the future of assetization.

NEW TOOLS ARE ENABLING DIY FINANCE

Alongside the opening up of access to private and alternative investments, investors like Ada are also gaining increasingly sophisticated tools to help them build portfolios their own way. This shift is empowering a new generation of self-directed investors—people who want to be more hands-on, making choices that reflect their own strategies, values, and interests rather than relying solely on advisors or prepackaged products. The result is a landscape where Ada can not only reach more assets but also exercise far greater freedom and control in shaping her financial future.

If opening up access to once-unattainable assets is, at least to some extent, like Spotify letting any musician share their music with the world, then the rise of self-directed investing is more like platforms such as Plex or Subsonic—tools that let listeners stream and organize their own music collections on their own terms. These platforms require a bit more technical skill and a hands-on approach, but in return they offer far more freedom and control than the mainstream alternatives.

This rise of investor autonomy is also an important part of the broader assetization story. It's not just about what you can invest in, but how you can invest—on your own terms, with far more freedom than ever before.

One of the initial catalysts for self-directed investing was the introduction of zero-commission trading. Until the mid-2010s, every time you bought or sold a stock, you paid a fee—usually $5 to $10 per trade, sometimes more. If you wanted to build a portfolio of just ten different stocks, you could spend $100 or more getting in and another $100 getting out. For anyone managing their own investments, these commissions were a real barrier, discouraging frequent adjustments and making it harder to experiment or rebalance.

Everything changed in 2013, when Robinhood launched commission-free trading. The idea was so popular that, within a few years, every major broker—Fidelity, Charles Schwab, E*TRADE, TD Ameritrade—followed suit. By 2019, zero-commission trading was the norm across all major platforms.

Another closely related development—and an important tool for DIY investors—has been the widespread availability of fractional shares. Put simply, fractional shares let Ada buy a portion of a stock or ETF, instead of having to purchase a whole share. This means that instead of needing thousands of dollars to invest in high-priced companies, she can allocate smaller amounts to any stock or fund she chooses.[11]

For Ada, this feature makes it practical to diversify her portfolio, even with a modest balance. She can invest $50 or $100 across a broad range of companies, spreading her risk without being shut out of expensive names. Fractional shares also allow her to fine-tune allocations or experiment with ideas that would have required a much larger account in the past. Alongside zero-commission trading, this is one of several tools that make hands-on investing much simpler and more accessible.

Robo-advisors are another important tool in the DIY toolkit. These are digital platforms that utilize algorithms to automatically build and manage an investment portfolio. They are a bit like music recommendation engines on Spotify: you tell them your goals and preferences—how much risk you're comfortable with, how long you want to invest, what you want to achieve—and the algorithm creates a personalized, diversified investment mix, usually using low-cost funds. It keeps things on track by automatically rebalancing your portfolio and can even help reduce your taxes by selling certain investments at the right times.

For Ada, the biggest difference from working with a traditional human advisor is cost and convenience. Where a human advisor might charge 1% of her assets every year (that's $1,000 annually on a $100,000 portfolio), robo-advisors often charge a quarter of that, or even less. The entire process is digital: Ada simply signs up online, answers a few questions about her goals and risk tolerance, and lets the algorithm handle the heavy lifting.

Not surprisingly, robo-advisors have taken off. Globally, they managed $1.4 trillion in 2024 and are expected to more than double by 2033.[12] In Europe and Japan, most financial institutions now offer robo options. In the United States, prominent names like Betterment, Wealthfront, and Vanguard manage hundreds of billions of dollars in this manner.

It's not always a choice between robots or humans, either. Ada—and many investors like her—often use hybrid approaches, combining algorithmic management with the option to consult a human advisor when needed. Many financial planning firms now use AI tools to enhance the efficiency and effectiveness of their services, rather than replacing personal advice altogether.

On the opposite end of the spectrum, investors who prefer a more hands-on approach can utilize direct indexing. This involves purchasing the individual stocks that comprise an index, rather than investing in an ETF or mutual fund that tracks the index.

If Ada wanted to own the S&P 500 using direct indexing, she would buy all 500 stocks individually, each in the correct proportion. At first glance, this might seem odd—why wouldn't she just buy an S&P 500 ETF? But direct indexing gives Ada significant advantages. She can customize her portfolio: leave out companies she doesn't want (oil stocks, for example, if sustainability is a priority) or overweight the sectors she believes in (for example, defense stocks, if she believes geopolitical tensions will drive value in this area).

Until recently, direct indexing was only for the wealthy, with buy-in minimums of $250,000 or more. However, new technology—such as fractional shares and zero-commission trading—has lowered the entry point to just a few thousand dollars.[13] By 2024, direct indexing assets had reached $864 billion, and the category was experiencing rapid growth.[14]

With direct indexing, investors can go beyond the standard menu of index funds—building a portfolio that reflects their own values, preferences, and tax needs, right down to the individual stock.

These and other tools are giving people much more agency in building their own portfolios—and if you believe the surveys, they're embracing it. Most self-directed investors believe their portfolios will perform as well or better than the market, and rather than being afraid of volatility, many of them view downturns as buying opportunities, not threats.[15]

THIS IS GOOD NEWS, BUT THERE'S A CAVEAT

Wave 1 has expanded what investors can access and how much control they have. Ada can now invest in private equity, infrastructure, private credit, and tokenized assets—all previously unavailable. She builds portfolios using thousands of ETF building blocks, fractional shares, and DIY tools. She decides sector exposure, geographic weighting, factor emphasis. The control sits with her.

This is progress. The industry has opened in ways that seemed impossible twenty years ago. Decision-making has moved toward investors. Choice has multiplied. Costs have dropped.

But there is a limit.

All of this expansion remains under institutional control. Investors can access more and control allocation, but they cannot create products. BlackRock decides which ETFs to launch. JPMorgan decides which private

"The industry has opened in ways that seemed impossible twenty years ago. But all of this expansion remains under institutional control."

market vehicles to build. Moonfare decides which funds appear on its platform. The gatekeeping has loosened. The gates remain.

The power dynamic has shifted without reversing. Institutions respond to investor demand. They compete by offering choice rather than imposing judgment. But creation—the actual manufacturing of products—stays institutional.

This matters because institutional menus, however vast, reflect institutional priorities: scale, profitability, regulatory comfort, operational efficiency. If something is too small, too complex, too niche, it won't get built. If it does, it will be structured for institutional convenience, not investor needs.

If you are an investor, it's important to understand that, despite all this access, your investment choices are still limited compared to what they could be. This however is set to change.

NOTES

1. ETFGI (2025). *Global ETF Assets Reach Record High of US$18.81 Trillion at End of September.* https://etfgi.com/news/press-releases/2025/10/global-etf-assets-reach-record-high-us1881-trillion-end-september (accessed 28 November 2025).
2. Reuters (2025). *Flows into US ETFs Cross $1 Trillion at Record Pace, State Street Investment Management Says.* https://www.reuters.com/markets/wealth/flows-into-us-etfs-cross-1-trillion-record-pace-state-street-investment-2025-10-14/ (accessed 28 November 2025).
3. Bloomberg (2024). *Wall Street Has Culled Some 1,000 Mutual Funds in Past Decade.* https://www.bloomberg.com/news/articles/2024-05-09/wall-street-has-culled-some-1-000-mutual-funds-in-past-decade (accessed 28 November 2025).

4. Milken Institute (2025). *Wealth Management: Merging Public and Private Market Strategies | Global Conference 2025.* https://www.youtube.com/watch?v=PTOhwjW5n9Q (accessed 28 November 2025).

5. Off the Charts (2025). *More PE Funds Than McDonald's.* https://offthecharts .substack.com/p/more-pe-funds-than-mcdonalds (accessed 28 November 2025).

6. Picard, Dan. (2025). *Evergreen Private Equity Funds.* https://www.morganstanley. com/im/en-ch/intermediary-investor/insights/articles/evergreen-private-equity-funds.html (accessed 28 November 2025).

7. Cantor Fitzgerald Asset Management (2025). *Interval Funds: Unlocking Access to Private Markets and Real Assets.* https://www.cantorassetmanagement .com/wp-content/uploads/2025/07/Cantor-Perspectives-Interval-Funds-Unlocking-Access-July-2025.pdf (accessed 28 November 2025).

8. CNBC (2025). *State Street, Apollo Team Up to Launch First-of-Its-Kind Private Credit ETF.* https://www.cnbc.com/2025/02/27/state-street-apollo-team-up-to-launch-first-of-its-kind-private-credit-etf.html (accessed 28 November 2025).

9. BlackRock (n.d.). *Bridging Public & Private Markets.* https://www.blackrock .com/us/financial-professionals/investments/bridging-public-private-markets (accessed 28 November 2025).

10. Capital Group (2025). *Capital Group and KKR Launch First Two Public-Private Investment Solutions.* https://www.capitalgroup.com/about-us/news-room/capital-group-kkr-launch-public-private-solutions.html (accessed 28 November 2025).

11. Forbes Business Council (2024). *The Rise and Reality of Fractional Investing: Why Education Is Essential.* https://www.forbes.com/councils/forbesbusiness council/2024/11/25/the-rise-and-reality-of-fractional-investing-why-education-is-essential/ (accessed 28 November 2025).

12. Yahoo Finance (2025). *Robo Advisor Market Projected to Reach USD 3.2 Trillion by 2033.* https://finance.yahoo.com/news/robo-advisor-market-projected-reach-143000875.html (accessed 28 November 2025).

13. Morningstar (2025). *The Direct-Indexing Landscape in 3 Charts.* https:// www.morningstar.com/funds/direct-indexing-landscape-3-charts (accessed 28 November 2025).

14. Cerulli Associates (2025). *Direct Indexing Assets Close Year-End 2024 at $864.3 Billion.* https://www.cerulli.com/press-releases/direct-indexing-assets-close-year-end-2024-at-864.3-billion (accessed 28 November 2025).

15. InvestmentNews (2025). *Amid Market Turbulence, Self-Directed Investors Keep the Faith, Study Reveals.* https://www.investmentnews.com/equities/amid-market-turbulence-self-directed-investors-keep-the-faith-study-reveals/261788 (accessed 28 November 2025).

Investing is shifting from a seller's to a buyer's market

For decades, large financial institutions decided what products existed. Today, the power dynamic is flipping. Thanks to ETFs, new digital platforms, and the convergence of public and private markets, investors have more choice than ever before. We are living through the industry's "streaming moment"—but there is still a limit.

Chapter Summary

- Historically, investing was a "seller's market": institutions decided the menu, and investors just picked from it.
- Today, it is becoming a "buyer's market": investors have the tools to decide their own allocation.
- The rise of ETFs was the industry's "streaming moment," unbundling the market into thousands of modular building blocks.
- Public and private markets are now converging, with major firms racing to democratize access to private equity and credit.
- New vehicles like evergreen funds and interval funds are lowering the barriers to entry for alternatives.
- Digital platforms are bypassing traditional gatekeepers, offering direct access to everything from art to infrastructure.
- DIY tools like fractional shares and direct indexing allow for hyper-personalization at low cost.
- The Limit: While investors can now access almost anything, the power to create products still belongs to the institutions.

"Assetization is about breaking down barriers and opening up investment opportunities to all. It is essential to democratizing finance."

Spiros Margaris, Margaris Ventures, Venture Capitalist and the world's No. 1 fintech and finance influencer and top AI influencer.

"Assetization is an innovative and bold endeavor and brings much needed innovation into financial markets. A new source of financing will further entrepreneurship."

Raymond J. Baer, Chairman of Alpine Select Ltd.

CHAPTER FOUR

WAVE 2—THE CONTAINERIZATION OF FINANCE

I n this chapter we explain how new infrastructure is collapsing the cost, time, and complexity of creating financial products. We use Malcolm McLean's containerization of shipping as the guiding analogy: standardization enabled global trade by making logistics trivial. In a similar way, financial containerization (securitization, tokenization) as well as the disaggregation, modularization, and standardization of the financial product value chain, is making financial product creation accessible to non-institutional players including the independent financial advisors and institutional wealth managers we are addressing in this book.

A QUIET REVOLUTION
AT SEA

On April 26, 1956, Malcolm McLean, an American businessman and owner of a successful trucking company, loaded 58 aluminum truck trailers onto a creaky old World War II–era tanker ship called the Ideal-X, moored in Newark, New Jersey. The ship set out on a five-day voyage to Houston, Texas. That small journey would mark a turning point in world history.

McLean was the inventor of what has come to be known as containerization—the practice of shipping cargo in standardized containers that can easily be loaded and unloaded onto various modes of transportation. Their use dramatically reduced costs and increased the speed and capacity of global shipping by road, sea, rail, and air.

McLean's idea didn't come out of nowhere, of course. The idea of designing special containers for cargo has a long pedigree. Many date it back to at least 1766, when James Brindley built a boat—the Starvationer—with wooden containers for coal built into the hull. This was a purpose-built vessel, also known as a "box boat,"[1] made specifically for the task of transporting coal around the canals of England, and the containers were designed with this task, and no other, in mind. Over the centuries, containers of various kinds have developed to cater to different cargoes and different modes of transport, be they ships, railroads, trucks, or aircraft.

This led to a global patchwork of custom-made containers. McLean realized this was putting the cart before the horse. The purpose of the logistics industry, as he put it, was not to "sail ships, but to move cargo."[2]

This led him to rethink the shipping process from the bottom up, looking at it from the perspective of the cargo rather than the vessel.

This change of perspective led him to conclude that what the industry needed most was not purpose-built ships for one kind of cargo but rather standardized containers for all types of cargo. And he was right. Standard-sized containers can be stacked efficiently, saving space. Built with standard locks and fittings, they can be easily loaded and unloaded between different modes of transportation—not just ships, but trains, planes, and trucks—and in different countries. All of this saves time and effort.

"Containerization has been credited not only with revolutionizing the shipping industry, but also with driving globalization. It truly changed the world."

And that, in turn, saves money. In 1956, it cost over $55 per ton (in today's currency) to load cargo onto a ship manually. Within fifty years, that had dropped to 21 cents per ton.[3]

While the outsides of shipping containers are standardized, the insides can be customized to accommodate different types of cargo. Today, we have containers for dry goods, refrigerated goods, liquids, perishables, fragile items—you name it. As long as the container conforms to the standards, transport companies can move it easily and efficiently from point A to point B.

This might not seem like much in and of itself. But containerization has been credited not only with revolutionizing the shipping industry, but also with being a prime driver of globalization during the second half of the 20th century. It has had an immeasurable impact on the global economy. When McLean died in Manhattan in 2001, Forbes magazine called him "one of the few men who changed the world."[4]

That was not an exaggeration.

THE INVESTMENT INDUSTRY IS CONTAINERIZING

We often tell this containerization story when people, particularly those outside the financial services industry, ask us to explain assetization. That's because assetization not only works on similar principles; we strongly believe that it will have as profound an effect on global investing as containerization has had on global trade.

And while, like all analogies, it may not be perfect, there are many parallels.

Containerization is a great example of the impact that modularizing and standardizing infrastructure can have. This was the case with shipping containers: by making the containers themselves a standard size and shape, it became much cheaper and easier to move goods anywhere in the world. Costs dropped dramatically, and suddenly anyone—not just big companies with their own ships—could send pretty much anything, anywhere. In that sense, it democratized global shipping. Sure, the post office always existed for small packages, but containerization allowed even small businesses to take advantage of the global transport system.

But containerization wasn't just about the containers themselves. The real transformation happened when the whole shipping infrastructure adapted. Ports installed new cranes, ships and trucks were redesigned, and warehouses and logistics networks were retooled. Much of this infrastructure already existed in some form, but it wasn't standardized or interoperable.

Something very similar has happened in the financial industry. Just as shipping containers standardized the packaging and handling of goods, securities arose as a way to standardize and then efficiently package and issue financial claims. And once these containers were in place, it paved the way

> *"We believe that assetization will have as profound an effect on global investing as containerization had on global trade."*

for full-scale financial infrastructure. Exchanges for buying and selling securities, custodians for keeping them safe, and the like. This kind of standardization has made it cheaper and hence easier for more and more people to participate in the investment industry.

We believe that this standardization has not yet run its course. In the previous chapter, we showed how the investment infrastructure is changing to give more people access to a wider range of assets. In this chapter and the next, we focus on the next step: how the forces of standardization and modularization are opening up the tools of product creation and distribution, so that many more participants can design, package, and bring financial products to market.

To make it clearer how this can work, we'd like to deep dive into the part of this value chain we know best: the containers.

SECURITIES ARE THE ORIGINAL CONTAINERS OF FINANCE

A security is a financial container—a wrapper for assets.

From a functional perspective, a security is, at its core, a contract. This contract defines a set of rights and obligations between parties, typically involving ownership of, or a claim to, an underlying asset or pool of assets. In other words, a security wraps something of value—a loan, a share of a company—inside a standardized legal agreement. The package can then be bought, sold, and traded in financial markets.

Just as early shipping containers came in all shapes and sizes before McLean, there were all sorts of ways to create agreements around claims before securities arrived on the scene: handwritten IOUs, local credit ledgers, bills of exchange, promissory notes, and one-off partnership contracts. What securities did was turn that patchwork of bespoke promises into standardized, fungible units that could move through a common market infrastructure, much like standardized containers finally let goods flow smoothly through ports, ships, trains, and trucks.

Thanks to a process known as "securitization," securities have also evolved from containers for single assets to ones that can hold large numbers of diverse assets.

Historically, that process has generally begun with a lender collecting similar loans or assets—such as mortgages, car loans, or credit card debt—and pooling them together. This pool of assets is then sold to a specially created entity called a special purpose vehicle (SPV), whose sole purpose is to hold and manage these assets separately from the lender's main operations.

An SPV is a legally distinct company that owns the assets and is structured so that, even if the original lender goes bankrupt, the assets in the SPV are protected from the lender's creditors. This asset isolation reduces risk for investors and is one of the main reasons SPVs are a crucial part of securitization. By separating the assets from the financial health and obligations of the originating bank, the SPV ensures that investors are exposed only to the performance of the pooled assets themselves, not to any unrelated troubles of the lender.

"Securitization is a powerful instrument, but it is complex, costly, and slow."

The SPV then packages the right to collect payments from this pool and issues securities—for instance, notes that investors can purchase and trade. Payments made by borrowers on the underlying loans flow through the SPV and are distributed to investors, who receive regular payments based on the pool's performance. Purchasing a mortgage-backed security in this system means investing in the collective monthly income of thousands of homeowners.

This process transforms illiquid single loans into a pool of assets wrapped in tradable investments that can be bought and sold in the market. This is the true "superpower" of securitization: the ability to transform assets that are difficult to trade—like loans or homes—into liquid, tradable securities. This liquidity not only benefits the institutions that originate loans but also helps broaden participation in financial markets.

While securitization is a powerful and very successful tool, there is room for improvement.

The process as practiced today is complex, costly, and slow, making it difficult for all but the largest banks and asset managers to participate. It's basically a "factory model": every transaction is custom-built from scratch, requiring teams of lawyers, bankers, accountants, and rating agencies to engineer each deal individually. The paperwork is immense, the regulatory and accounting requirements are strict, and the process can drag on for months. Legal, accounting, and administrative fees quickly add up. In fact, unless you have a very large pool of assets—often $50 million, $100 million, or more—the transaction costs will wipe out most of the benefits. For smaller players, the barriers are so high that most banks and arrangers won't even take a meeting for deals under a certain size. Securitization simply isn't practical for the vast majority of asset owners. In effect, this old-school model is completely pre-McLean: everything is bespoke, nothing is standardized, and only the biggest institutions can afford to take part.

One other note: While we said that in classic securitization, assets are isolated inside an SPV, meaning investors are exposed only to the performance of the underlying assets and not to the financial health of the original lender, the reality is a bit more nuanced. In practice, banks often retain some exposure to the assets—for example, by holding the riskiest tranche or providing guarantees. Regulatory and accounting standards are also strict about when assets can truly be moved off the bank's balance sheet. As a result, it's not uncommon for some of the risk to remain with the bank, or for bank-issued products to carry counterparty risk. In other words, not all securitizations are created equal: in some, counterparty risk can be a real concern.

TOKENS ARE THE FINANCIAL CONTAINERS OF THE FUTURE

If securities are the traditional containers of the financial system, tokens are their digital-native counterparts. A token is a standardized digital wrapper for value, rights, or claims—one that moves along blockchain rails rather than traditional banking infrastructure. Just as a security is a legal container whose contents can vary widely, a token is a technical container whose internal content is equally flexible. The container is standardized; its contents do not need to be.

Importantly, a token is not a different legal category of asset. It is, as mentioned, a digital representation of rights or claims. Legally, a token can even be a security if it embodies the same rights as a security. The distinction is architectural: a security defines the legal contract, while a token defines the digital representation of those rights and how they travel through the blockchain infrastructure.

The original blockchain-based token was Bitcoin, the world's first viable form of decentralized electronic cash. (Indeed, the blockchain itself was invented specifically to make Bitcoin work—more below.) Because the blockchain software was open source, it was easy for others to copy and adapt it.

Soon after Bitcoin appeared, other tokens followed—Litecoin, Namecoin, Dogecoin, and countless others. These early tokens were simple. Just as in the early days of securities, where one share represented one claim, early tokens represented only a single type of value.

This changed with the arrival of Ethereum, a new kind of blockchain that introduced smart contract capability. A smart contract is self-executing code on a blockchain that defines how a token behaves. This made tokens programmable containers. Instead of being tied to their own single-purpose blockchains—as every bitcoin-inspired coin required, since each one meant copying and modifying Bitcoin's code—tokens on Ethereum could be created directly through smart contracts and run on the same shared infrastructure. Ethereum also introduced standardized token formats so that all parts of the infrastructure, wallets, exchanges, and applications, could recognize and work with new tokens instantly.

"We can think of tokenization as the digital equivalent of securitization."

Smart contracts also made it possible to embed rules and automated behaviors directly into the token itself—governing how it moves, when it can be transferred, how revenues are distributed, or how it participates in digital processes such as governance. In short, programmability transformed tokens from simple units of value into flexible, interoperable building blocks for a new kind of financial infrastructure.

The process of using a smart contract to "containerize" a right or claim and issue it on a blockchain in the form of a token is known, unsurprisingly, as tokenization. We can think of tokenization as the digital equivalent of securitization.

One of the most important use cases for tokenization today is to represent claims to off-chain assets on a blockchain in order to take advantage of the portability, programmability, and efficiency of blockchain infrastructure. This approach is commonly known as the tokenization of real-world assets, or RWA.

These off-chain assets can be just about anything of value in the real world. Tokens can represent rights to tangible assets such as real estate, art, fine wine, or commodities; rights to financial exposures such as loans, treasury bills, or fund interests; or rights to intangible assets such as intellectual property. The category of underlying asset doesn't really matter. What matters is that the rights associated with it are encoded in a smart contract and issued in the form of a token.

Tokenization points toward the next generation of financial infrastructure. By turning rights to almost any asset into programmable digital containers, it promises a world where value can move as easily as information across a shared, global network. Large players are already leaning in: major asset managers are exploring tokenized funds and other products as a parallel, and potentially eventual primary, rail for financial markets.

For now, however, tokenization still involves considerable friction. Legal enforceability for real-world assets, fragmented technical standards, uneven regulation, and clunky user experience all mean that issuing a tokenized product is still closer to a bespoke project than to the plug-and-play container world McLean created. In that sense, tokenization today remains "pre-McLean": powerful in principle, but not yet supported by fully standardized, universal infrastructure.

But this is changing fast.

PUTTING THE CONTAINERS TO WORK: THE GENTWO EXAMPLE

To show how the infrastructure of investing is changing at the product-creation level, let's take a closer look at GenTwo.

As outlined in Chapter One, GenTwo started life in response to the nagging friction in securitization. As a true fintech, we approached the solution in classic tech fashion: by standardizing, modularizing, digitizing, and automating.

The first step was to break down the securitization value chain into component parts. As we've seen, one component is the security itself, which acts as the container. Another component is the container's interior, which must be capable of holding the specific financial cargo being placed in it. Like physical containers, which can be fitted with refrigeration equipment or adapted to hold liquids, various financial structures can be used inside the security for different purposes—actively managed certificates, tracker certificates, credit-linked notes, and the like. For our purposes, it's not necessary to get into the details of how these work. What was important was creating a process to easily and cost-effectively match the right interior to the container, depending on the client's goals.

Another component was the SPV (see above). The GenTwo team developed a process that allowed clients of any stripe to easily set up their own SPV and become issuers of their own products. As you may recall from Chapter One, this idea—letting clients themselves become the issuers instead of relying on banks—was one of the things that ruffled feathers when we first announced it. We like to think of this as one of our major innovations, because at the time creating own issuers for clients wasn't very common. But it was key to making the product creation process as independent as possible.

The next step was figuring out how to let clients actually make use of these capabilities. To do this we built a digital platform called GenTwo Pro.

GenTwo Pro is a platform designed as a one-stop shop to allow clients to easily build and issue a financial product without the need for a bank. Like any other such platform, it works via a digital interface. Once logged in clients and can request new products or monitor existing ones.

If it's a new product, the client fills out a form which gathers the basic information on their idea—they choose the underlying assets, the product type, fees, terms, and the product's life. This sets into motion all the structuring, legal, KYC, compliance, and other processes necessary to get the job done.

Since the platform also serves as a digital workflow engine as well, clients can easily monitor the whole process and help shepherd the product to completion. The platform also allows the client to easily monitor performance, issue instructions (e.g., payments), and otherwise administer their product and interact with the GenTwo team.

Once a new product is ready, it can be packaged—that is, placed in a container so it's ready to ship.

Most products are packaged as traditional securities. They receive an ISIN—an official securities number—so they can be issued on an exchange. Once that's done, investors—generally clients of the client—can purchase certificates.

However, they could just as easily—and increasingly are—be packaged as a token. The preparation work is generally the same. The difference is that, by being tokenized, the product is placed in a container that runs on blockchain rails. It is also possible to package a product as both a security and a token to leverage the capabilities of both traditional and digital infrastructure.

We like to think that there are several advantages to the approach we have taken.

First, it can be done for any asset, for example niche commodities like uranium or art; or for any strategy, for example AI-driven equity portfolios. There are basically no restrictions on what can be securitized. Whether it's a traditional investment, a niche asset, or an entirely new idea, the platform is designed to handle it. As Patrick likes to say, we provide a blank canvas, and clients paint on it what they want.

Second, it's cheaper and more efficient than traditional securitization. That's because, thanks to our technology, our unit costs are much lower than those in a large institution.

An important by-product of this is that the system works just as well for smaller-ticket items as for large ones. There's no need to come with a

$100 million deal and convince a bank that it's worthwhile for them to issue your product.

Ours is also an open platform in that clients can, at least to varying degrees, choose their own component parts—counterparties, partners, providers. By design, there is no "vendor lock-in," no being stuck with whatever a single bank or provider offers. This frees users from the dependency that comes with the big securitization factories.

This is classic platform-building: taking the existing elements and standardizing them to put the tools into the hands of users, using an open rather than a closed architecture, and democratizing the process by making it available to—and viable for—users of any size.

But financial product creation is only one part of the investment industry value chain.

Just like the shipping infrastructure needed to be updated before containerization could work its magic, so too there are other parts of the investment industry infrastructure being updated now as well. The value chain is being disaggregated, modularized, and—most importantly—opened up, turning what used to be closed, vertically integrated systems into open platforms on which many different creators can build. There is important precedent for just how powerful such processes can be.

UNEXPECTED REVOLUTIONS

As we saw with McLean, significant technological or infrastructure innovations often come as a surprise. They have unexpected benefits or unfold in ways their creators did not originally intend and have impacts far beyond what they set out to do.

Consider these two stories.

In the mid-2000s, Apple set out on a secret mission to reinvent the phone. Steve Jobs gathered a select team, directing them to combine the music player, the phone, and the internet communicator into a single device. They succeeded, launching the original iPhone to wide acclaim; it was sleek, intuitive, and packed with technical innovation. But Jobs had drawn a line—third-party developers were to be kept at bay, limited to making web apps that could run through the browser. It was a stance he defended fiercely, worried about security and control.

Yet, outside Apple's walls, tinkerers found ways to break through, creating unauthorized applications and showing a hunger for more. Gradually, Apple yielded. The App Store opened, suddenly making the iPhone a platform open to anyone with an idea. Seemingly overnight, developers transformed the device, spawning new industries and reshaping daily life. Ride-sharing, messaging, photo sharing—all these and more took root, none imagined on launch day. The true revolution emerged not from Apple alone, but from the unexpected energy released once the tools were handed to others.

In the late 2000s, a pseudonymous programmer or group of programmers under the name of Satoshi Nakamoto wanted to solve an old problem: how to create viable digital cash without banks or other trusted authorities. Drawing on decades-old concepts of cryptographic chains and decentralized systems, Satoshi assembled something new—a chain of data blocks, linked and secured, kept honest by countless independent participants. Bitcoin was born, its fortunes rising among a small circle of enthusiasts. The code was made open and available to anyone willing to experiment.

Over time, others took notice. As already mentioned, the underlying blockchain, meant only to record Bitcoin transactions, was repurposed—

first for new digital coins, then for running automated contracts and even tracking supply chains. Its openness sparked waves of innovation, each branching further from Bitcoin's intended purpose. Today, blockchain has become the shared infrastructure for digital assets, identities, and systems that Satoshi likely never imagined.

We are telling you these stories to make a point: What seem like radical breakthroughs are, in reality, often just a question of rethinking and remixing existing ingredients in new ways. And the inventors of true breakthroughs are often not even aware of their true significance until others come along.

> *"New technologies tend to have the most impact when they are open."*

There are a few things that we find interesting about stories. First, both Jobs and Nakamoto were not necessarily inventing new things from scratch: they were, for the most part, remixing existing technologies and rethinking the approaches to the problems they were trying to solve, though each added their own innovations on top as well.

More significantly, we'd argue, both of these innovations only took off and had big-time, global impact because they were open. In Jobs' case, this openness had to be forced on him. In the case of Bitcoin, the code was open source from the start. That left the door ajar for others to step in and continue the innovating: all the app builders on the iPhone, the creators of new blockchains, coins, smart contracts, and all the other advances that have turned blockchain technology from a libertarian experiment into what very well could become the new backbone of the global financial infrastructure. We would also point out that, as a result, these technologies had a profound democratizing effect. They put power and capability into the hands of individuals, with understandably profound effects.

HOW THE INVESTMENT PRODUCT VALUE CHAIN IS BEING DISRUPTED

With this as a backdrop, let's take a look at how the investment product value chain is currently being opened up.

The investment industry infrastructure consists of many interconnected parts. For public markets, most of this infrastructure is highly developed, although it has traditionally been vertically integrated within large "universal" or full-service banks that created products, distributed them, and managed custody, settlement, and reporting internally. What's interesting from an assetization perspective is how this is evolving as fintechs and other new entrants break apart the value chain and expand it into private markets, alternatives, and real assets.

For example, at the manufacturing layer, securitization, structured-product, and tokenization platforms provide the legal, operational, and technical infrastructure to package assets or strategies into standardized financial containers. What once mainly existed within large, vertically integrated institutions is increasingly available as modular services—such as issuance vehicles, documentation templates, risk engines, and digital workflows—that external users can access. This reduces minimum size requirements and broadens product creation to a wider array of participants. This is the work of GenTwo and many of our peers.

Once products exist, distribution infrastructure determines who can access them. Historically, distribution was dominated by proprietary channels: institutions manufactured products and pushed their own shelves to captive clients. Today, open-architecture and platform-based models aggregate a broad universe of funds and alternative products and make them available through unified digital interfaces. In parallel, new platforms are expanding access to private-market and other alternative assets, either serving investors directly or acting as toolkits for advisors and intermediaries. The net effect is a shift from closed, institution-centric pipelines to open, platform-centric ecosystems that broaden access and choice. See for example Allfunds or Moonfare.

Below the surface, custody, settlement, and asset servicing form the core plumbing. Custody ensures safe, segregated holding of assets; settlement makes transfers final and reliable; servicing handles income, corporate actions, record-keeping, and reporting. These functions were long concentrated in a small group of global institutions and geared to very large clients. Over time, specialist administrators and service providers have made back-office and fund-administration capabilities available "as a service," and digital-asset custodians have extended institutional-grade controls to blockchain-native instruments. When real assets are securitized or tokenized, existing specialist storage and logistics infrastructures can be connected to financial structures so that everything from commodities to collectibles can be held and serviced using similar operational frameworks. See for example global fund administrators and custodians such as Apex Group, digital-asset custody platforms like Anchorage Digital, and specialist real-asset providers such as Crozier in art storage.

Trading venues and secondary marketplaces are where these containers change hands. Public markets rely on exchanges, order books, and standardized clearing and settlement to provide continuous price discovery and liquidity. Private markets, by contrast, have traditionally relied on bespoke, bilateral negotiations with limited liquidity and long lock-ups. New secondary platforms introduce more standardized listing, matching, and settlement workflows for private assets, making it easier to organize periodic auctions or structured transactions rather than reinventing the process deal by deal. This brings a degree of repeatability and transparency to areas that were previously illiquid and opaque. Examples include private-share marketplaces such as Nasdaq Private Market and Forge

Global, token-based venues for private assets such as ADDX, and fractionalized-asset platforms that let investors trade slices of real estate (Arrived) or collectibles like art (Masterworks).

Valuation, pricing, and data providers supply the information layer across this chain. Asset-specific valuation is handled by auditors, administrators, and specialist appraisers who establish fair value for companies, properties, infrastructure, intellectual property, and other real or financial assets. On top of that, analytics and data platforms compile information on deals, performance, flows, and market conditions, allowing investors to benchmark opportunities and compare managers or strategies. Public markets benefit from continuous prices and standardized reporting, while private markets now have far richer datasets than in the past, even if they still fall short of full transparency. Together, certified valuations and structured data make a much wider set of assets analyzable and investible. Examples include valuation specialists such as Kroll and private-markets data platforms such as PitchBook and Preqin.

Finally, lifecycle, regulatory, and compliance technology increasingly bind the value chain together. Lifecycle-management tools orchestrate events such as rebalancing, roll-overs, notifications, and reporting across multiple intermediaries. Regtech and compliance systems automate know-your-customer checks, anti–money-laundering monitoring, suitability assessments, and regulatory reporting, reducing manual work and making it feasible to handle larger product universes and more granular client customization. As these layers become more automated and interoperable, the entire value chain shifts from a patchwork of institution-specific processes into a more standardized, modular infrastructure—exactly the environment in which assetization can flourish. Here for example you'd find AI-driven AML and screening platforms such as ComplyAdvantage, digital identity and KYC providers such as Veriff, and lifecycle-orchestration and compliance tools embedded in fund platforms and portfolio management systems.

FINANCIAL PRODUCT CREATION IS BEING DEMOCRATIZED

When we started this chapter, we used containerization to illustrate how an industry can transform when its fundamental components become standardized. Since then, we've traced the development of securitization, distribution, custody, trading, valuation, lifecycle systems, and compliance—showing how that logic unfolds in finance. As the value chain breaks down into parts that can work together, it becomes more open and accessible.

Openness is what turns standardized infrastructure into a factory anyone can use. When structuring, issuance, custody, trading, and reporting are available as modular, on-demand services rather than being locked inside a few vertically integrated institutions, many more professional users can assemble and launch products without owning the whole factory.

Here history can serve as a guide. In publishing, standard digital formats, on-demand printing, and global storefronts broke the value chain into services any writer could tap, so authors could become their own publishers. In e-commerce, payment gateways, storefront platforms, and fulfilment services modularized what used to be end-to-end retail operations, so anyone with an idea could become a merchant. In technology, cloud computing turned servers, databases, and analytics into standardized, pay-as-you-go building blocks, so anyone could be a developer. The same pattern of standardization, modularization, and openness is now unfolding in finance, turning product creation from a vertically integrated privilege into a toolkit that many more participants can use.

In the next chapter, we show how this modular, open infrastructure sets the scene for radical automation of the value chain. And how that is when things can become very interesting.

NOTES

1. Wikipedia (2025). *Containerization*. https://en.wikipedia.org/wiki/Containerization (accessed 14 February 2026).
2. Ibid.
3. Foundation for Economic Education (2025). *Malcolm McLean: Truck Driver, Entrepreneur, Billionaire*. https://fee.org/articles/malcom-mclean-truck-driver-entrepreneur-billionaire/ (accessed 14 February 2026).
4. Ibid.

Investment infrastructure is transforming

Just as the standardized shipping container revolutionized global trade by decoupling the cargo from the ship, standardized financial containers are revolutionizing investment. But the container is just the tool; the real revolution is the disaggregation of the banking infrastructure that supports it.

Chapter Summary

- In 1956, the shipping container revolutionized global trade by standardizing how cargo moved.

- Finance is undergoing a similar transformation: the "containerization" of investment products.

- Securities (and now tokens) act as standardized wrappers that allow any asset to move on financial rails.

- Standardization and modularization is happening across the whole investment product value chain.

- Infrastructure is shifting from a monolithic "factory model" to modular, interoperable components.

- This dramatically lowers the friction and cost of issuing new financial products.

- Independent advisors and smaller firms can now access the tools of issuance without needing a bank's balance sheet.

- The monopoly on product creation is breaking, allowing the "buy side" to become the "sell side."

"With Assetization, we see how advanced technology combined with an infinite and creative mindset can break down silos, reduce friction, democratize access to opportunity, and unlock value. This will enable a fairer and more transparent financial system for everyone."

Tim Grant, CEO, DeusXCapital

"Assetization is the catalyst for an open and digital ecosystem in which any asset becomes tradable and bankable. It empowers financial institutions to orchestrate clients and partners across industries - unlocking innovation, broadening opportunity, and delivering client value at unprecedented scale."

Dr. Daniel Fasnacht, CEO & Founder of EcosystemPartners AG.

CHAPTER FIVE

WAVE 3—RADICAL AUTOMATION

I n this chapter we look ahead to the third and most radical wave of assetization: the full automation of the product lifecycle. Starting with a futuristic vignette set in an art gallery, we illustrate a "prompt-to-product" world where AI agents handle structuring, legal, and compliance in seconds. We then provide a picture of a future where investment marketplaces become universal, the distinction between buy side and sell side dissolves, and almost any verifiable value—from art collections to industrial machinery—can be seamlessly turned into an investible asset. Whether you are an investor or an advisor, this future represents a completely new paradigm. We start with our vignette, in which our friend Barbara meets her gallery owner friend Clemens.

IN THE GALLERY

The sculptures catch the light like frozen music. Abstract forms in polished bronze, each taller than a person, are arranged throughout the gallery's white space. Champagne glasses clink. Voices murmur in that particular pitch of opening night conversation—half genuine admiration, half networking.

Barbara finds Clemens near the back, standing beside the largest piece. She congratulates him on having taken over the representation of Alfred Tithon, the world-famous sculptor. Quite a coup. He thanks her but confesses that working with this level of artist is not as easy as people think. He gestures around the room. Each piece, he explains, sells for a minimum of $500,000. Some much more. They've valued this whole series at ten million. There's always an incredible amount of effort involved finding buyers at these price points. It's a waiting game.

Barbara smiles and pulls out her phone.

"How would you like to sell the whole thing this week," she asks.

Clemens laughs. "Now how would I do that?"

"By not selling whole pieces to individual collectors," she answers, "but rather packaging the whole collection as an investment product and selling shares to investors."

"Okay," Clemens answers, looking incredulous and interested at the same time. "How would something like that work?"

"Let me show you," she answers and pulls out her phone.

"Do you mind if I take a picture?" Clemens nods in agreement.

Barbara steps back, frames all ten sculptures in the viewfinder of her phone, and taps the screen to shoot the picture. Then she opens an app on the phone.

"Watch this," she says.

The app opens with a subtle chime and the GenTwo agent greets her in a pleasant AI voice. She explains she's at the Clemens Wyse gallery for the opening of Alfred Tithon's new sculpture series. They'd like to assetize the collection. She asks the agent if it knows about the artist. The response comes immediately: "Yes, quite a well-known figure."

Barbara sends the photo. "We think the series is worth ten million at a minimum." She asks the agent to analyze the viability of securitizing the collection.

The screen changes. Text scrolls past: processing image, checking external sources, researching Tithon price history, checking art market forecasts, querying proprietary product data, analyzing GenTwo product database for similar structures, reviewing Barbara's distribution history, creating recommendations.

Clemens leans closer. "What's it doing?"

"It's figuring out if our idea will work," Barbara says.

In less than a minute the agent returns. It tells them it thinks it likely that the collection will appreciate in value meaningfully over the short- to mid-term, making for an attractive investment. We can expect high demand. It also recommends an initial valuation of twelve million.

Clemens blinks. "Twelve?"

Barbara nods and asks if he wants to do it. Clemens agrees, and Barbara tells the agent to proceed.

The screen changes again: structuring agent creating term sheet, legal agent drafting contracts, compliance agent running digital verification, marketing agent preparing materials, issuance agent creating security, smart contract agent minting a token. Twenty-seven seconds later the product package is ready.

The system asks them to review. Barbara and Clemens swipe through the screens—legal documents, term sheets, marketing materials with professional photos of the sculptures, distribution plans.

"Shall we move forward?" she asks. Clemens, looking a bit dazed, says yes.

When everything is ready, she hands the phone to Clemens for his signature. "Your thumbprint will do," she says. He presses his thumb to the screen.

The agent continues processing for a few seconds. Then it provides the following update: the product has been published to Barbara's distribution network: push notification sent to nearly three thousand qualified investors. It has also been added to GenTwo's online marketplace. The token has been minted and listed on affiliated exchanges.

Barbara's phone buzzes. The first subscription has come in: that's $200,000. She tells Clemens they should be fully subscribed by the end of the week, based on past performance with similar products. He stares at her.

"That's amazing," he says.

"No, that's assetization," she answers with a smile.

THE THIRD WAVE OF ASSETIZATION IS RADICAL AUTOMATION

The vignette above is based on a video we created in the summer of 2024 to illustrate a thesis we were developing about how assetization could evolve. You can view the video on our book website.[1]

Before we explore the reasons behind this vision, we want to clarify that it was just a thought experiment, something we initially did for ourselves (although we later published the video). More importantly, we are technologists, not art market experts. Therefore, we leave it to the reader to judge how realistic or unrealistic our underlying gallery scenario is.

That said, we do feel confident in our thesis, which is that the final wave of assetization—the end game of the processes we've described so far—is complete automation of the entire financial product lifecycle.

In the previous chapter, we demonstrated how the financial product lifecycle has gradually been broken down. Each phase—structuring, legal, compliance, marketing, issuance—has been separated and offered as a specialized function. When an industry's value chain becomes modular, standardized, digital, and built from interoperable components, automation shifts from just a possibility to a likely outcome. It becomes the next logical step.

That is what we tried to capture in our video.

If you look at our original storyboard, you can see this in action. The scenario posits a product creation app. We allowed ourselves to make it a GenTwo app, but it could have come from anyone, and we expect that, in the future, there will be many such apps. This app consists of an AI agent and a number of sub-agents who represent the specialists needed to make a product.

Once the user, in this case Barbara, queries the agent, the process begins.

Part I of the process is product ideation. The agent queries external sources for publicly available information on the artist, including previous sales history. It also checks price trends for similar artists' works, broader art market data, and relevant forecasts.

Next, it searches GenTwo's proprietary database for the history and performance of similar products created by GenTwo clients, along with how those products were marketed and distributed. This non-public information is closely guarded and remains confidential. Only the agent has access to the full overview. With this perspective, the agent can draw on GenTwo's product experience to assess the viability of the idea, the likelihood of finding investors, the structures and terms that tend to work best, and even suggest pricing.

"The natural endgame of assetization is automation. It's the vibe coding of financial products."

Since Barbara is a long-standing client, the agent also reviews her previous products, the types of investors she works with, their buying history, and the performance of her offerings.

85

From all this, the agent makes its recommendation.

Part II is product creation. Once the agent gets the go-ahead, it sets the sub-agents to work. There's a structuring agent that structures the product and generates the term sheet. There's a legal agent to write the contracts. The compliance agent handles due diligence—these days, that often means online checks or a quick fingerprint scan for ID. The marketing agent puts together a marketing plan, creates a product video, and prepares other materials. Each specialist does its part.

Crucially, the sub-agents work in parallel. That's what makes the process fast. In the video, everything is done in under thirty seconds. That may sound bold, but we wanted to make a point: radical automation will mean radical speed.

The final step is approval and launch. The agent returns with the term sheet, contracts, marketing materials—everything ready to review. Once Barbara and Clemens are satisfied, Clemens confirms. The product is issued, opened for subscription, and marketed. It's available in at least two ways: as a bankable note and as a token. In the not-too-distant future, we think such hybrid offerings will be the norm. Further out, it may only be tokens.

Within five minutes, the first investor comes in. This, too, may be somewhat optimistic on our part, but again, we are trying to make a point.

Certainly if you look around the industry today you can see hints of this already happening. AI has played an essential role in financial services for years, and companies are increasingly employing genAI and AI agents to automate tasks. This will only increase. And AI is already moving into the area of financial product creation, if in baby steps. One recent report from an AI vendor claimed that in the structured products world, agents could already "analyze client-specific data—investment goals, risk tolerance, and portfolio holdings—to generate optimal structured product configurations," reduce "the time needed for product customization from hours or days to seconds," analyze "past deals and market trends to identify high-performing payoff structures" and the like.[2]

Admittedly this isn't exactly securitizing a real asset in less than 10 seconds, but it gives a sense of the direction of travel.

We like to think of this in terms of different analogies.

One is 3D printing. When 3D printing emerged, it democratized manufacturing in a specific but powerful way: the means of production that once required a factory floor could now sit in a garage or on a desktop. You could design something, send it to a printer, and have a physical prototype in hours instead of weeks. The complexity of the manufacturing process became embedded in a machine and software. What changed was who could access it.

Another, perhaps more apropos, analogy is vibe coding, which refers to the use of AI agents to create computer code including complete applications from simple prompts. The user doesn't even need to know how to code.[3]

So we ask ourselves, if a non-programmer can tell an AI to "build a responsive music app" and have working software delivered in minutes, then why can't a wealth manager tell an AI agent to "structure a diversified art collection as an investment product" and have term sheets, legal documents, compliance checks, and marketing materials ready for review just as quickly?

Our thesis is that this will become possible. And as these tools improve—as the kinks get worked out—the barrier to entry for product creation will continue to fall.

AUTOMATION WILL TRANSFORM THE INVESTMENT LANDSCAPE

If "prompt to product" does become a reality, the next obvious question is what this all means. We've been thinking about this as well and have come up with a set of four general predictions that we think outline the shape of the industry as these capabilities come online. They are as follows:

Advisors and Wealth Managers Will Have Access to Tools to Create Products Themselves

As tools for creating financial products become more accessible to professionals, their democratization advances. Capabilities once limited to the product factories of large banks will increasingly be available directly to wealth managers, asset managers, and advisors. This is a natural result of a value chain that has been modularized, digitized, and opened up: when each component exists as an interoperable service, the barriers to using it fall. The outcome is not a world where everyone designs financial products, but one where the professionals already doing this work can access far more powerful tools than before.

"Instead of calling structurers, waiting for legal teams, or coordinating with compliance officers, they engage with AI agents."

For Barbara and Clark, creation becomes something they do through direct interaction with intelligent platforms rather than long chains of human intermediaries. Instead of calling structurers, waiting for legal teams, or coordinating with compliance officers, they engage with AI agents that interpret their intent and turn it into concrete product proposals. Their experience of creation becomes more conversational: they describe the outcome they want—"a lower-volatility version of this strategy," "a product that suits my client's liquidity needs"—and the system assembles the relevant components behind the scenes. Developing a new product no longer means moving through multiple departments with their own queues and timelines; smart systems handle those steps in parallel, so Barbara or Clark can try out ideas, test scenarios, and refine structures in minutes instead of days.

This new creative freedom still operates within the realities of a regulated industry. Financial product development will continue to require licensed professionals who understand their obligations and work within clear boundaries. Regulation, suitability rules, fiduciary duty, and the economics of distribution ensure that these tools remain in the hands of trained intermediaries rather than the general public—at least initially.

Investment Marketplaces Will Become Open and Universal

If the creation of financial products becomes more accessible, their distribution will likely follow. Once professionals like Barbara and Clark can generate new ideas quickly and at low cost, those ideas need a place to go. The natural destination is large digital marketplaces where products can be listed, discovered, compared, and bought—a meeting point between creators and investors in a world no longer limited by a few institutions.

A useful—if imperfect—analogy is e-commerce: platforms like Etsy or Shopify, with thousands of storefronts, broad catalogues, and powerful discovery tools. Investment marketplaces will share this feel—diverse shelves, creator-driven supply, rich search—but will operate within financial regulation rather than as anything-goes bazaars. They will be professional, supervised environments that borrow the openness and variety of digital marketplaces.

> *"The natural destination is large digital marketplaces where products can be listed, discovered, compared, and bought."*

Supervisory authorities will still decide who can invest in what, what disclosures are required, and what qualifies as suitable for a given investor. The marketplace's role is to automate these rules: verifying eligibility, embedding risk warnings, enforcing suitability, maintaining audit trails, and restricting access where needed. Regulation sets the boundaries; the platform makes those boundaries seamless and largely invisible.

For investors, these marketplaces will feel like smart discovery tools. They can filter opportunities by asset class, location, risk level, impact, theme, or return profile, and follow specific creators—professionals like Barbara or institutions like Clark's bank—whose offerings match their interests. Advisor agents can surface relevant products based on a client's portfolio and stated goals, making the investible universe searchable, personalized, and easier to navigate.

For professionals, the marketplace becomes a powerful new distribution channel. Instead of relying only on proprietary shelves or limited client lists, creators can showcase offerings where qualified investors are already searching. Niche ideas that were too specialized for a single bank's platform can find an audience in a larger market. Barbara gains visibility for bespoke exposures; Clark's institution can test different expressions of its house views and adapt quickly to real-time demand signals.

Everyone Can Become a Seller

So far, we have argued that the new creation tools will remain primarily in the hands of financial professionals, and this will remain true for the foreseeable future. But if automation continues to advance, the line between "professionals" and "everyone else" will begin to blur. Once product creation is largely automated and compliance, structuring, and documentation are built into the tools themselves, the ability to issue an investment product shifts from being mainly about financial engineering expertise to mainly about whether a credible asset or cash flow is available.

In such a world, small and mid-sized businesses can access financing options that were once reserved for large institutions. A manufacturing

> *"In such a world, small and mid-sized businesses can access financing options that were once reserved for large institutions."*

company might issue revenue-sharing claims tied to the output of a specific machine; a software firm with recurring subscriptions could offer instruments backed by defined streams of contract revenue. The same logic extends beyond finance and into the real economy more broadly—something explored in more detail through concrete use cases in the next chapter.

None of this implies that individuals will casually engineer complex products on their own. Even as issuance becomes more accessible, the rails it runs on remain supervised, with regulation increasingly embedded in the process. Professional intermediaries—wealth managers, asset managers, banks, or eventually automated agentic systems governed by regulatory standards—will continue to provide oversight, suitability checks, and investor protection. Over time, however, some of the functions that Barbara and Clark perform today may be executed increasingly by machines, even if the responsibilities themselves do not disappear.

Seen through this lens, "everyone can become a seller" does not mean that financial engineering becomes a hobby. It means that businesses, creators, communities, and organizations with real economic activity can access capital markets in ways that were previously out of reach, with issuing a product becoming as operationally straightforward as running payroll or invoicing because complexity is handled by agentic systems within regulatory boundaries. This is the outer horizon of assetization: as costs fall and automation deepens, the long tail of the economy can be financed through regulated, AI-mediated channels, making the system more inclusive and flexible and softening the boundaries between capital markets, community funding, and private investment.

Everything Can Be Made Investible

As the mechanics of product creation become faster and more automated, it becomes possible to imagine a world in which almost anything of value could be made investible. Not everything will be, and not everything should, but the capability is what matters. The untapped-assets side of this story—the private companies, long tail of economic activity, and adjacent asset classes—is explored in more detail later in the book.

Here, the point is simpler: once you can take a verifiable cash flow, price it, document it, and distribute it through a regulated channel, the investible universe expands in unexpected directions. A musician's future royalties, the subscription revenues of a software business, or the output of a single machine on a factory floor all become conceptually investible once the friction of creation is removed.

There is a clear upside. A larger investible universe means more ways to diversify, spread risk, and direct capital to places it could not reach before. Small businesses that struggle to access loans could raise money on the strength of the revenues they already produce; creators could fund their work on reasonable terms; communities could finance local infrastructure. Much of this activity is too small or idiosyncratic for traditional finance to bother with. Automation changes that by allowing the system to reach deeper into the real economy.

> *"A larger investible universe means more ways to diversify, spread risk, and direct capital to places it could not reach before. But there are limits to what should be assetized."*

But an expanded universe also brings new risks. Not everything of value should be turned into an investment product, even if the tools make it possible. Some things simply do not belong on a balance sheet: certain claims on essential public services, for example, can raise sharp economic, political, and moral questions when converted into tradable rights. There are categories of highly sensitive personal data that most people would not want to see bundled and sold, no matter how elegant the structure. And there are corners of the economy—gray or outright criminal—that would gladly use financial engineering to create a veneer of legitimacy if given the chance. These are real boundaries and acknowledging them is part of being honest about what assetization can and cannot do.

Beyond that lie more ordinary dangers: mispricing, thin-market manipulation, over-promised yield schemes, or straightforward fraud. When new types of assets become investible, they also become targets. Fraudsters thrive in moments of transition, when trust can be manufactured faster than understanding, and the same tools that lower barriers for legitimate issuers can lower them for bad actors as well. Investors may overestimate their grasp of new structures, while enthusiastic founders or creators may take on obligations they later regret. More access also means more room for misjudgment, especially when the tools make everything appear simple.

All of this places regulation and supervision at the center of the story. For this future to work, regulation will likely become more important and more deeply embedded in the machinery. Regulators set the boundaries of what is permissible; platforms, agents, and marketplaces enforce those boundaries automatically. If everything runs on code and the rules are baked in, these systems could, in some respects, be safer than what exists today.

The tools make almost anything investible. The harder and more important question is what we choose to make investible. That choice will determine whether this expanded universe becomes a source of opportunity or a source of problems, and—as with every major shift in finance—the decisions made now will shape what this frontier looks like when the next wave of innovation arrives.

WAVE 3 REPRESENTS A FUNDAMENTAL CHANGE

This future is still emerging. Our vision remains speculative—a projection based on current trajectories rather than documented reality. But if this is indeed the direction of travel, the implications are profound.

The boundaries between different players in the investment world begin to blur. For investors, choice expands dramatically but so does complexity—navigating an almost limitless universe of investible assets requires either sophisticated judgment or trusted guidance. For advisors and wealth managers, full automation appears to threaten disintermediation. Yet history suggests the opposite can also be true: in worlds of unlimited choice, demand for curation and advice intensifies rather than disappears.

For advisors and wealth managers, the critical question isn't whether this future arrives, but whether they position themselves to benefit from it. In the next chapter, we make the case for why they should.

NOTES

1. For the video and other information around this book, visit www.assetizationbook.com.
2. Grid Dynamics (n.d.). *Structured Products: Harnessing AI-Driven Digitalization*. https://www.griddynamics.com/blog/structured-products (accessed 28 November 2025).
3. Wikipedia (2025). *Vibe Coding*. https://en.wikipedia.org/wiki/Vibe_coding (accessed 28 November 2025).

The future is radical automation

If Wave 2 is about standardizing the infrastructure, Wave 3 is about automating the workflow.

We are heading toward a "prompt-to-product" world where AI agents handle the heavy lifting of structuring, compliance, and issuance in seconds. This will expand the investible universe to include almost anything of value.

Chapter Summary

- The industry is moving from "industrial" standardization to "radical" AI-driven automation.
- Prompt-to-Product: In the near future, creators will design compliant financial products via natural language interfaces.
- Structuring, legal work, and compliance checks will move from taking weeks to taking seconds.
- Embedded regulation will ensure that rules are baked directly into the code, not checked manually.
- Universal marketplaces will connect niche creators with global liquidity, similar to e-commerce platforms.
- The definition of "asset" will expand to include revenue streams, intellectual property, and industrial output.
- Small businesses and communities will gain access to capital markets previously reserved for corporate giants.
- The Challenge: An expanded universe brings new risks, requiring smarter supervision to prevent fraud.

CHAPTER SIX

FROM CURATOR TO CREATOR

I n this chapter we make the case that assetization offers advisors and wealth managers a way forward. By breaking down the barriers to financial product creation, it allows them to move from curators to creators—building their own products instead of merely selecting from someone else's shelf.

This shift addresses multiple pressures at once: advisors can differentiate their offerings, recover margins, retain assets that might otherwise drift to competitors, and most importantly, reclaim control of the client relationship. The tools exist. The question is whether they'll be used.

But first, we take a quick look at the state of assetization today.

PUTTING TOGETHER THE FORBES ASSETIZATION LEADERS LIST

In the previous chapter, we discussed ideas for the distant future of assetization. But where are we today?

In the spring of 2025, we decided to find out. And so we partnered with Forbes Switzerland to create an Assetization Leaders List. The idea was to identify people and projects outside our orbit that were driving the changes we have been discussing and to gauge assetization through an independently managed process.

The response was very encouraging. Forbes received over 200 applications from asset managers, technology platforms, infrastructure providers, and others, all tackling assetization-related challenges. The Forbes jury (including Philippe) ultimately narrowed the candidates to a 30 person list.

The list makers can be broadly divided into three categories.

Some were involved in creating new types of assets: fractionalizing collectibles; structuring museum-quality art portfolios; transforming football clubs into investible vehicles; tokenizing agricultural revenues; and packaging employee health and public-sector debt as assets.

Others focused on building the supporting infrastructure: a blockchain-agnostic platform that enables banks to issue and manage digital assets securely; AI-automated onboarding and compliance; and an independent platform for small firms to issue and trade equity directly.

A fair number of established financial institutions applied as well. One offered a regulated investment vehicle that connects mainstream investors to digital assets. Another was opening access to private markets for a wider audience. A third was automating the issuance of structured products. There was also a project to integrate crypto into private portfolios and another to expand ETF distribution by blending conventional and digital offerings.

It was encouraging to see so much assetization-relevant innovation on display.

For Barbara and Clark, this is good news. Here's why.

ADVISORS TODAY ARE CAUGHT IN A SQUEEZE

Life is not easy these days for independent advisors and wealth managers. A quick search for "state of the wealth management industry" yields studies and data outlining a sector under siege from many directions, driven by multiple factors.[1]

One big one is fees. In a world of low-cost ETFs, zero-commission trading, and other low-cost options, it becomes harder for advisors and wealth managers to justify what they charge. At the same time, costs are rising, driven largely by compliance, which requires expensive specialists and heavy IT investment. This eats into revenue.

It is also harder for advisors and wealth managers to differentiate themselves and prove their value add. This is hurting their brands. When an advisor recommends a BlackRock or Vanguard fund, clients often wonder why they need the advisor at all. Why not just buy the fund directly? In this world the advisor can look like an extra layer of fees while providing what amounts to standard market performance.

At the same time, clients expect more from them. As we have seen, younger investors are losing patience with the established ways of doing things.

They want faster service, digital solutions, and access to alternative and exotic assets. Wealth managers need to adapt to this, which is not always easy or cheap.

We are also living through a period of great change and uncertainty. Markets are volatile. Old certainties are being questioned. Investors across the board are looking for guidance and more personal attention. Providing that attention requires time and infrastructure. Custom service comes at a cost.

> *"It is harder for wealth managers to differentiate themselves and prove their value add."*

In theory, this need for guidance should make advisors and wealth managers more valuable to investors. But while it is one thing to provide personalized advice, it is another to have the tools to implement it. That is where, in our opinion, the problem lies.

As the industry has evolved, with the rise of mass-market digital platforms and open architectures, the wealth manager has become a curator of other people's products. Even when advisors have specific insights about what their clients need or see opportunities in the market, they are usually limited to selecting and combining existing products rather than creating new ones. Those products are now readily available to investors directly.

We have seen this movie before. Travel agents once thrived as trusted guides until airline websites and booking platforms made it possible to buy flights directly, often more cheaply. Independent bookshops and record stores were valued for their curation, but mass platforms like Amazon and Spotify overwhelmed them with endless, cheap choice.

Wealth managers risk following the same path. As investment products become more accessible and platforms more sophisticated, the value of simply selecting from existing options diminishes. To remain relevant, advisors need to offer something the platforms cannot—not just better curation, but genuine customization.

Assetization can address this and the other issues facing advisors and wealth managers by letting them transition from being curators to, when appropriate, being creators of financial products. By creating their own products, they can differentiate themselves and justify their fees. By building solutions that match what clients actually want—including alternatives and exotic assets—they can meet rising expectations without sending assets elsewhere. And by putting the advisor's brand on the investment itself, they can finally capture value instead of handing it to fund manufacturers. The benefits of this shift look different depending on where you sit in the industry.

ASSETIZATION HAS BENEFITS FOR BARBARA

As a creator, Barbara could finally stand out again. For years, she has been offering the same funds and products as everyone else. It has not mattered how hard she worked or how well she understood her clients—when the investments all came from the same handful of manufacturers, her value disappeared into someone else's brand. By creating her own solutions, she could show her thinking directly. A client would open their statement and see something she built, reflecting her judgment. That alone puts her in the foreground instead of the footnote.

Barbara could also protect her business from fee pressure. Today, she is pushed to recommend cheap, mass-market products. The moment she does, she enters a race she cannot win. No human advisor can compete on price with platforms that deliver baskets of ETFs at near-zero cost. When she creates something of her own—something that reflects

"As a creator, Barbara could finally stand out again."

a real idea and a real need—she is no longer compared to an app. She can charge fairly for work that is actually hers. She earns her margin again.

Barbara could take back control of the client relationship. Right now, most of the credit goes to the big names printed on the products she rec-ommends. Even when she has done the work—understanding the client, shaping the portfolio, managing behavior—the brand value flows outward. By creating, she becomes visible again. The client sees her on the page. Her name carries the idea. That builds loyalty in a way no amount of quarterly calls ever could.

She could also act much faster when she sees a pattern forming among her clients. Maybe several families start asking about clean-energy pro-jects. Maybe younger clients mention the same new technology. Maybe a local business community is excited about a regional opportunity. In the old world, all she could do was explain that nothing on the product shelf matched those conversations. Now she can respond. She can build some-thing that reflects a shared interest across her clientele—not for one per-son, but for the group of clients who clearly care about the same thing. Trends that used to slip through her fingers can become investible ideas. In other words, Barbara could finally start saying "yes."

This could help Barbara grow her business instead of watching assets leak away. When she recommends an external fund, the money effectively leaves her orbit and strengthens someone else's franchise. When she creates something herself, those assets stay connected to her. They remain part of her platform and become the foundation for long-term relationships. What used to be outflows becomes part of her own ecosystem.

And Barbara could do all of this without becoming a technician. She does not need to be an engineer or a structurer. The infrastructure handles the heavy lifting. She gets the kudos.

Most importantly, Barbara could regain her purpose. She became an advisor to guide people, not to fill in forms and pass along the same dozen products. Creation puts her judgment back at the center. It allows her to be the professional she intended to be: someone who listens, understands, designs, and protects.

ASSETIZATION HAS BENEFITS FOR CLARK

Clark works at a private bank. He cannot just start whipping up new products on a whim—there are processes, compliance, research committees, and all the usual institutional machinery. But Clark is not blind. He sees what is happening: younger clients are experimenting elsewhere, assets are trickling out to competitors, and if nothing changes, his bank risks sliding into irrelevance.

Assetization gives Clark a fighting chance.

The secret is partnership. Clark can push his bank to team up with specialist platforms—firms that already know how to structure and deliver these new solutions. Private banks rarely build complicated issuance infrastructure in-house. Instead, they lean on trusted partners to handle the heavy lifting, while the bank does what it does best: steward client relationships, ensure governance, and handle custody. Modern financial product creation platforms fit this model.

That also helps solve the research bottleneck. Most banks require full internal coverage before advisors can pitch a product. With a vetted partner platform, the bank does not need to scrutinize every single structure. It sets the rules, then lets advisors tap into a broader menu of options.

Clark's real edge is that he is the one talking to clients every day. He hears the requests his bank cannot currently meet—private-market access, alternative strategies, tailor-made structures. He spots patterns long before a product committee does. Clark can translate what his clients want into language his institution understands:

"Here is what we are missing. Here is where we are losing out. Here is a low-risk way to catch up."

He can propose pilots, narrow use cases, defined client segments, and clear suitability rules. Prove the model in miniature, then scale. This is how private banks actually innovate: cautiously, via partnerships, with oversight at every step.

"Clark's real edge is that he is the one talking to clients every day."

Once these partnerships are in place, Clark wins. He can finally say "yes" to client requests instead of apologizing for internal limitations. He keeps clients who might otherwise walk. He shores up his bank's relevance.

Clark will never have the same freedom as Barbara, but he does not need to. He has institutional backing, governance, and stability. The partnership model lets him gain agility without sacrificing those strengths. Banks that adapt keep advisors like Clark in the game. Those that do not watch their best clients—and people—walk out the door.

Clark's job is to make the case and to do it before time runs out.

OTHER SECTORS OF THE FINANCIAL INDUSTRY CAN BENEFIT

There is no reason why the tools of assetization should be confined to wealth management. Here are some use cases in other sectors of finance.

Hedge fund managers could bring strategies to market without launching full funds. A manager who has developed a promising approach but does not have the time or scale for a full-blown fund could package that strategy in a simple, regulated format. This would let them raise capital more quickly and test an idea with real investors without waiting months for a fund to be built. For clients, it means earlier access to strategies they previously never saw. For advisors, it means more variety—but also more competition.

Venture capital firms could share individual opportunities without creating a new vehicle every time. If a firm has a compelling investment in a young company and a group of investors who want in, it could structure that single opportunity cleanly and offer it without weeks of legal work. Investors could participate with lower minimum commitments, and the firm could move at the pace the deal demands. This benefits investors and gives advisors something new to offer.

Private equity managers could let investors participate in specific deals rather than only through large, closed-end funds. If a firm wants to finance a new purchase, it could structure a simple product tied to that one deal. Investors would know exactly what they are entering, and the firm could raise the additional capital it needs when it needs it.

Managers working in private markets could bring opportunities to investors in ways that were simply not possible before. These managers sit on real assets—infrastructure projects, renewable-energy installations, real-estate portfolios, private-credit deals—that are often compelling but locked inside large, slow structures. Capital has to wait for the next fund. Investors have to accept long lockups, high minimums, and limited visibility. It is an industry built around the idea that everything has to be big, negotiated, and time-consuming.

If the machinery becomes lighter, that assumption no longer holds. A manager overseeing a wind farm or a solar development could package the economic exposure to that project in a straightforward, bankable format. Instead of waiting for a full fundraising cycle, they could raise capital when opportunities arise. Instead of offering only a multi-year closed-end fund, they could create a smaller product tied to a specific project or group of projects. Investors would know exactly what they are exposed to, and the manager could move at the pace of the underlying asset rather than the pace of traditional fund administration.

The same applies to real estate or private credit. A manager who sees an attractive property acquisition or a portfolio of income-producing loans could bring that exposure to market far more quickly. They would not need the full apparatus of a new fund; they could structure a product that tracks the cash flows directly. Lower minimums and faster onboarding would bring these opportunities to a broader audience without changing the underlying assets or watering down their quality.

Firms working in the digital-asset space could translate complex on-chain strategies into formats ordinary investors can use. Many digital strategies generate returns in ways that are technically difficult for most people to access—such as earning yield from network participation or providing liquidity to online marketplaces. These firms could keep the complexity behind the scenes while offering the economic results in a form that sits inside a regular account. The strategy remains on-chain, but the investment behaves like familiar financial exposure. This lowers the barrier for anyone who wants to participate in digital assets without dealing with wallets, private keys, or specialized systems.

They could also bring more sophisticated payoffs to digital assets, not just simple exposure. Until now, most crypto products have amounted to buying a token and hoping it goes up. With the right tools, a firm could design outcomes that look more like the structured solutions available in traditional markets: partial protection against losses, accumulation features that help in sideways markets, or payoff profiles that reward moderate, steady growth. These formats are well established in currencies and commodities. Extending them to digital assets gives investors a way to engage with the space more cautiously and selectively.

Some investment platforms could turn product creation into a natural extension of the services they already offer. Those that already combine custody, trading, and basic investment workflows are well placed to add creation tools on top. They already handle most of the operational work around holding assets, moving money, and reporting. Allowing their users to assemble simple products within the same system would be a logical extension rather than a radical departure. What used to require a long list of external providers could, in time, be handled in one place.

Larger institutions could take a similar approach. Instead of building every structure internally, they could work with outside partners who handle the technical side while the institution focuses on governance, client relationships, and safe custody. This would let them move faster without changing the parts of their business that are built for stability. In effect, product creation becomes another service layer rather than a specialized department buried deep in the organization.

NON-FINANCIAL FIRMS CAN BENEFIT

The story does not stop with financial firms. Once the machinery becomes lighter, it is not only advisors, asset managers, or banks who can act on their ideas. The same tools open the door for businesses outside finance as well.

Many small and mid-sized businesses run solid operations but hit the same wall when they try to grow: getting funding when they need it. Banks take a long time and want piles of paperwork. Equity investors can feel like the wrong fit for owners who want to stay in control. A local brewery that wants to add tanks, a neighborhood bakery that finally finds the perfect second location, a family-run food maker that needs better equipment—these are strong businesses slowed by a funding system that does not match how they actually work. With simpler

"Once the machinery becomes lighter, it is not only advisors, asset managers, or banks who can act on their ideas. The same tools open the door for businesses far outside finance as well."

creation tools, each of them could take one specific plan and turn it into something people in the community can invest in. Supporters would know exactly what they are backing, and the business would pay them over time based on how well that project performs. The owners stay in charge, the process moves at the pace of real life, and the experience feels closer to how these businesses naturally grow.

Manufacturers often face a basic problem: the machines they need to grow are expensive and buying them outright can drain cash. Borrowing to pay for equipment pushes risk onto the business before it has produced anything. Because of this, many factories delay upgrades or keep old machines running far longer than they should. With more flexible tools, a manufacturer could bring in outside investors to buy the machine and then pay for it gradually based on how much they actually use it. When production is high, payments rise; when production slows, payments slow too. It turns an intimidating upfront purchase into something closer to pay-as-you-go. The business gets the equipment it needs without a single large financial hit, and investors get a clear link between their support and the work happening on the shop floor. It is a simpler, more natural way to match financing with real activity.

Artists often deal with uneven income: months with plenty followed by months with very little. When they need money to start a new project, they usually face two choices: wait or take deals that cost them ownership or creative freedom. A musician who earns steady streaming income, a writer with reliable royalties, or a painter who regularly sells prints could use that future income to raise money today without giving up their rights. With simpler tools, they could turn part of their future earnings into a structure supporters can invest in. The artist gets the funds they need to start or continue their work. Supporters get to back someone they believe in and share in the income over time. Nobody signs their life away, and the creator stays in charge of their path.

ASSETIZATION IS A MAJOR OPPORTUNITY FOR THE BUY SIDE

To sum up: The disaggregation of product-creation infrastructure—the modularization we traced in the previous chapter—means advisors who understand their clients' needs can now respond by building solutions rather than searching for approximations on someone else's shelf. In other words, the buy side can increasingly become the sell side as well—and encroach on its turf.

This shift puts independent advisors and wealth managers—the Barbaras and Clarks of the world—at a rare juncture. They face two opportunities: one professional, one commercial. The first is the chance to serve clients better by expanding what is possible. The second is the chance to build stronger businesses by breaking free from commoditization.

"The buy side can increasingly become the sell side as well—and encroach on its turf."

We think they should seize both.

A Chance to Serve Better

First, there is the opportunity to do a better job for clients. Assetization is expanding what is possible in investment: more assets are investible, more exposures are accessible, and new channels are opening. This should be a moment of professional pride. Clients are navigating more options and more complexity than ever before, and the value of skilled, trustworthy guidance has only increased.

As toolmakers, we see how today's infrastructures let advisors break out of old constraints and add new dimensions to their practice. When the toolkit grows, so does the advisor's ability to respond to real client interests. The tools now exist to say "yes" more often and more precisely: to design solutions that closely match what individual clients care about and to help investors put their money behind ideas that matter, not just what is listed on someone else's shelf.

Advisors and wealth managers can use assetization to make their work more meaningful: deeper personalization, quicker responses to emerging trends, and the chance to help clients invest in the ideas they truly believe in. Those who embrace this expanded role become more relevant, not less. The trust built from thoughtful service grows stronger in a world of almost unlimited choice. Genuine guidance becomes a premium.

A Chance to Build Better Businesses

Second, assetization offers advisors and wealth managers a new way to fight back against the forces that threaten their relevance—the middleman squeeze we discussed above, with its fee pressure and slow erosion of value add.

For years, advisors have faced structural limits: recommending similar products, losing control over client relationships, and watching margin and loyalty drift away. The rise of direct platforms and standardized products has not only commoditized investment advice but also made it difficult for good advisors to differentiate on substance.

Assetization flips this dynamic. Armed with the right tools, they can break free from the standardized product shelf. They can create and deliver offerings that reflect both their expertise and the specific needs of their own clients. It is a real chance to add tangible, distinctive products to their offering and, in doing so, recapture the margin and brand recognition that slip away when recommending someone else's solution.

There is also a strategic benefit: personalized products anchor clients to the advisor, not just to the product provider. Loyalty follows substance, and substance is easier to create than ever. A business model built on tailored solutions is not just about volume or scale. It is about clarity, identity, and an authentic differentiation that stands up in a crowded market.

Crucially, assetization means advisors do not need to invest heavily or re-engineer their practice to begin. The cost and complexity of trying something new—from launching targeted opportunities to testing specialized products—have never been lower. Small steps matter, and early adopters have the chance to lead the field, shaping the advisor's business in ways that were out of reach only a few years ago.

NOTE

1. We also wrote a white paper on the subject ourselves. GenTwo (2025). *Product Shelf Syndrome: The Silent Crisis Facing Asset Management.* https://www.gentwo.com/articles/product-shelf-syndrome-the-silent-crisis-facing-asset-management/ (accessed 28 November 2025).

Advisors must evolve from curators to creators

The shift in infrastructure presents a massive commercial opportunity for wealth managers. By using the new tools of assetization, advisors can stop being allocators who curate other people's products and start becoming architects who build their own. This is the key to surviving the "middleman squeeze".

Chapter Summary

- Advisors today are "curators of other people's products," which makes it hard to prove their value.
- They face a "middleman squeeze": fees are under pressure, costs are rising, and differentiation is disappearing.
- Assetization flips the script: democratized tools allow advisors to become creators.
- For Independent Advisors (Barbara): Creation allows them to stand out, charge fairly for their work, and take back control of the client relationship.
- They can respond to trends quickly—turning a shared client interest into an investible idea.
- For Institutional Advisors (Clark): They can use partnership models to bring innovation inside the bank.
- This allows them to say "yes" to client requests for alternative strategies instead of apologizing for internal limitations.
- Ultimately, this is a chance to build a better business by offering distinctive products that clients can't get anywhere else.

"Assetization can bring transparency and discipline to emerging markets such as climate finance—and accelerate the move toward a more sustainable global economy."

Peter McKillop, Founder & Editor, Climate & Capital Media

"Assetization will fundamentally reshape how investors interact with new asset classes. It is the bridge between traditional finance and the new world of tokenized value."

Dr. Daniel Diemers, Co-Founder SNGLR Group

CHAPTER SEVEN

UNTAPPED ASSETS: THE TRILLION-DOLLAR OPPORTUNITY OF ASSETIZATION

n this chapter we attempt to quantify the sheer scale of the assetization opportunity. Moving beyond the shrinking world of stocks and bonds, we tour the vast landscape of "untapped" value, including private equity, private credit, infrastructure, real estate, and passion assets. By providing rough estimates of these markets, we show that the majority of the world's wealth sits outside the public exchanges, waiting for the right infrastructure to unlock what could be hundreds of trillions of dollars in investible value.

THE VAST MAJORITY OF VALUE SITS OUTSIDE PUBLIC MARKETS

Up to this point, we have argued that more and more of the economy is being pulled into financial form: private companies, real estate, infrastructure, digital claims, even passion assets. That should mean more diversification and more opportunities for investors to put their capital to work—but how much is actually out there?

In this chapter we try to put rough orders of magnitude on the answer. To be clear, these are very much back-of-the-envelope calculations, not precise forecasts and certainly not investment recommendations. Our goal is simply to indicate potential size. For each of the asset classes below, we therefore looked for reasonable estimates of the total addressable market (TAM)—the pool of value or the documented funding gap—and treated that as the reservoir from which assetization could draw.

We are not forecasting how much of that can or will actually be securitized or tokenized; the aim is simply to show that once you look beyond listed stocks and bonds, the numbers involved become very large very quickly.

REAL ESTATE—PLACES OF VALUE ($393 TRILLION)

Real estate is the original asset. Long before stock markets or bonds, wealth was measured in land and buildings. It remains the most intuitive investment there is: a tangible place that generates rent, keeps pace with inflation, and physically exists in the world. It covers everything from suburban homes and city-center apartments to shopping centers, warehouses, offices, hotels, and farmland—the spaces where people live, work, and produce.

It is also, by far, the largest store of wealth on the planet.

According to Savills, the total value of global real estate reached nearly $393.3 trillion at the end of 2024, split into $286.9 trillion of residential property, $58.5 trillion of commercial real estate, and $47.9 trillion of agricultural land.[1] To put that number in context, it is roughly three times the size of all the world's stock markets combined.

Yet for such a massive asset class, it remains remarkably difficult to access efficiently. For most investors, "investing in real estate" means buying their own home—a concentrated bet on one street in one city.

This is changing, if slowly. Today, the "financialized" slice of the market—where you can invest without buying the whole building—is tiny. Listed Real Estate Investment Trusts (REITs) hold roughly $2 trillion globally.[2] Professionally managed private real estate funds add another $3.8 trillion.[3]

Add it up, and the professionally managed universe is just under $6 trillion. It's a start, but still represents only roughly 1.5% of the global stock. The rest of the $393 trillion is still up for grabs, and gives us an upper bound for our total addressable market.

PRIVATE EQUITY— VENTURES OF VALUE ($60 TRILLION)

When people hear "private equity," they often picture giant buyout funds taking public companies private. In practice, most of the action is in ordinary, unlisted businesses: regional logistics firms, niche manufacturers, software providers, healthcare groups. These are real companies with real cash flows, just ones whose shares never make it onto an exchange.

In order to assess the total addressable market of private equity, it makes sense to look at the pool of such businesses. It is large. While there are roughly 44,000 listed companies in the world,[4] the total number of companies globally is estimated at 359 million.[5]

Most of these are small local businesses—cafes, plumbers, freelancers—that will never be targets for global capital. So of all those millions of companies, how many could be considered investible and thus potentially be assetized?

One answer comes from estimates by Scientific Infra & Private Assets (SIPA), a private-markets data firm spun out of EDHEC Business School. Using its proprietary private Metrics database, SIPA says that it has identified on the order of 900,000 to one million private companies worldwide that are large and transparent enough to sit in an "investible" private-equity universe, with a combined equity value of around $60 trillion—more than ten times the assets currently managed by global private equity funds. For our purposes, this provides a plausible proxy for the total assetizable private equity market.[6]

PRIVATE CREDIT—VALUE IN LENDING ($30 TRILLION)

If private equity is about ownership, private credit is about the engine room of the economy: the loans that keep businesses running.

For most of the 20th century, this was the exclusive preserve of banks. If a mid-sized manufacturer needed to buy a new factory, or a logistics firm needed to finance a fleet of trucks, they went to their bank manager. But since the 2008 financial crisis, that door has been slowly closing.

Stricter capital rules (specifically Basel III and now Basel IV) have forced banks to de-risk their balance sheets.[7] Holding capital against loans to small and medium-sized enterprises (SMEs) became expensive. So banks retreated, focusing instead on mortgages and lending to the largest, safest corporate giants.

This retreat left a massive void. Millions of viable businesses—the "missing middle" of the global economy—have found themselves starved of capital.

This vacuum has created an opportunity for private credit. Unlike private equity, which involves buying companies, private credit is about making loans—filling the lending gap that banks left behind.

According to McKinsey, for instance, the size of the addressable market for private credit in the United States alone could be over $30 trillion.[8] This jibes well with a recent survey by PwC.[9] In the absence of reliable estimates for the rest of the world, we will take the US-centric $30 trillion as our number.

INFRASTRUCTURE— FOUNDATIONS OF VALUE ($15 TRILLION)

Infrastructure is the essential framework that supports daily life. It includes the power grid that supplies electricity, data centers that process digital communications, roads and highways that enable the movement of goods and people, and water systems that deliver clean water to cities and towns. These systems operate continuously, providing the foundation for modern society.

For most of the post-war era, financing this was simple: the government paid for it. But that model is breaking down. Public balance sheets across the world are stretched by post-pandemic debt and the rising costs of aging populations. Governments increasingly lack the fiscal space to fund the massive upgrades the world needs—particularly the trillion-dollar transition to green energy and the explosion of digital infrastructure.

This has forced a profound shift. Infrastructure is moving from a public good funded by taxes to an investible asset class funded by private capital. Investors are now helping to build the wind farm or the fiber network, and in return, they get decades of steady, inflation-linked cash flows.

But money isn't moving fast enough.

The Global Infrastructure Hub—a G20 initiative set up to track this specific problem—estimates that the world needs to invest $94 trillion in infrastructure by 2040 to keep pace with economic growth and climate goals. Based on current trends, according to this source we will fall short by a staggering $15 trillion.[10] Therein lies an assetization opportunity too.

CRYPTOCURRENCIES— TOKENS OF VALUE ($10 TRILLION)

No discussion of alternative assets today can omit cryptocurrencies. At their best, they point to something genuinely new: Bitcoin as a potential digital store of value outside the traditional system and Ethereum as a programmable base layer where money, contracts, and assets can all run on the same rails. This vision of borderless, always-on, composable finance is what draws many of the smartest people in the industry into the space.

The path there, however, has been anything but smooth. In just over a decade, crypto markets have swung through spectacular booms and brutal busts, and high-profile episodes of fraud, hacks, exchange collapses, and energy-intensive mining have left a long shadow over the asset class. Whether one leans toward the promise or the problems, cryptocurrencies have become a serious, if controversial, part of the alternative asset universe.

For assetization, the question is less "good or bad?" and more "how big could this pool become if it matures?" The opportunity here is twofold.

First, there is adoption. If Bitcoin cements its role as "digital gold" and Ethereum (or other programmable blockchains) becomes the settlement layer for the world's financial contracts, the value of these networks could grow by orders of magnitude.

Second, there is utility. Some digital assets now generate yield, can serve as collateral, and enable new types of on-chain transactions. They're evolving from speculative tokens into productive assets.

How much is all of this worth from an assetization perspective? Today, the entire crypto market fluctuates between $2–4 trillion.[11] Some sources suggest the crypto market cap could reach around $10 trillion by 2030 as institutional adoption matures.[12] We think that this makes a reasonable number. As cryptocurrencies are easily accessible to all, the whole market is assetizable.

PASSION ASSETS—VALUE WITH MEANING ($2 TRILLION)

There are also assets we buy not just for return, but for love. "Passion assets" cover everything from Basquiat paintings and vintage Ferraris to rare Burgundies, Patek Philippe watches, and even game-worn sports memorabilia.

Historically, this was the ultimate "alternative" investment—unregulated, opaque, and strictly for the ultra-rich. The appeal is obvious: these are tangible objects that offer aesthetic pleasure and, crucially, have historically had low correlation with the stock market. A Picasso doesn't care what the Federal Reserve does with interest rates.

But as a financial asset class, it has always been deeply inefficient. Buying a blue-chip painting requires millions of dollars upfront. Selling it involves auction houses that take 20% commissions and months to settle. Storage and insurance eat into returns. It is the definition of "lumpy," illiquid wealth.

The market, however, is large. According to Deloitte, the overall value of art and collectibles holdings among ultra-high net worth individuals is just over $2 trillion.[13]

The opportunity here is not about creating new value, but about unlocking what is already there. It is about turning "storage wealth"—value that sits gathering dust in a vault—into active capital. Making these assets even marginally more liquid or accessible would represent a massive expansion of the investible universe.

FRONTIER ASSETS—NEW KINDS OF VALUE (<$0.5 TRILLION)

Beyond these major categories lies a set of emerging experiments that hint at where things could go next. These are not yet large or standardized markets—some remain highly speculative, others are just beginning to take shape—but they are worth noting because they show how far the definition of an asset can stretch.

Consider future cash flows. The famous "Bowie Bonds" of the 1990s securitized David Bowie's future music royalties, giving investors exposure to his catalogue's earnings. Similar structures have been used for film rights, patent royalties, and sports contracts. The logic is straightforward: if something generates predictable income over time, that income stream can be packaged and sold. What was once niche and bespoke is now scaling up: cumulative issuance of music royalty-backed securities exceeded $8 billion from 2020 to 2024, with $3.5 billion issued in 2024 alone,[14] and Concord's 2024 securitization—backed by catalogues containing over a million songs—was more than three times oversubscribed.[15]

Prediction markets offer another intriguing possibility. These platforms allow people to bet on the outcome of future events—elections, sporting events, even business decisions—by buying and selling contracts whose payoff depends on what happens. The resulting prices reveal collective expectations and in some cases have outperformed polls as forecasting tools. Polymarket, the largest decentralized prediction platform, processed over $9 billion in trading volume in 2024, with $3.6 billion wagered on the US presidential election alone.[16]

Then there is personal data and behavior. Data about what we search, buy, watch, and whom we know has already helped create gigantic corporations, yet most individuals have no direct way to monetize their own digital exhaust. Some technologists and academics imagine a future where people can package and sell their browsing history, social graphs, or movement patterns; the technical building blocks exist, even if the social and ethical case is far from settled.

Sports betting represents yet another expanding frontier. The global sports betting market exceeded $100 billion in 2024 and is projected to nearly double by 2030.[17] Most people think of this as gambling rather than investing—but the infrastructure looks surprisingly similar. Sophisticated bettors use statistical models and risk management techniques that wouldn't be out of place at a hedge fund. The difference is mostly one of framing and regulation. As these markets mature and become more transparent, the boundary between betting and trading may continue to blur.

Even more speculative are ideas like tokenizing reputation, intellectual property that has not yet been created, or future earning potential. Some of these concepts probably should remain thought experiments. But together, these examples—cultural, informational, probabilistic, reputational—show how many kinds of value people are trying to quantify, package, and trade once the tools exist to do so. For assetization, the point is not that every frontier should become mainstream, but that the frontier itself keeps moving: as the infrastructure for making things investible spreads, new categories will continue to appear at the edges of what portfolios can hold.

What's striking about all these examples is how they stretch the definition of what can be an asset. Each represents some form of value—cultural, informational, probabilistic, reputational—that someone, somewhere believes can be quantified, packaged, and traded. Not all of these experiments will succeed. Many probably shouldn't. But they serve as reminders that the frontier is not fixed: once you have the infrastructure to make things investible, new categories will keep appearing at the edges.

Taken together, these frontiers matter because they expand the very idea of what a portfolio can hold. For investors, they open paths to diversification that go beyond the familiar mix of stocks and bonds—into private markets, hard assets, digital value, and conviction-driven themes. For asset managers and advisors, they create the opportunity to respond to client demand with new products rather than recycled ones, and to differentiate in an industry that risks commoditization. The result is not a promise of instant liquidity or guaranteed returns, but something more enduring: a vastly richer set of building blocks with which to shape portfolios around risk, opportunity, and belief.

THE ASSETIZABLE UNIVERSE ($255 TRILLION)

The numbers above are almost unfathomably large. To recap, we have discussed:

- Real estate: a $393.3 trillion global stock.
- Private companies: an estimated $60 trillion universe of unlisted firms, the majority of which remain inaccessible to all but a narrow class of professional investors.
- Private credit: a $30 trillion addressable market of corporate, consumer, and asset-backed lending in the US alone that has only just begun to migrate out of bank balance sheets.
- Infrastructure: a $15 trillion funding gap that pension funds, insurers, and sovereign wealth funds are eager to fill—if the products exist.
- Crypto and digital assets: a market that *could* reach $10 trillion by decade's end.
- Passion assets: $2 trillion of art, wine, and collectibles held by ultra high net worth individuals, a sliver of which is already moving onto fractional ownership platforms.

- Frontier assets: music royalties, prediction markets, personal data, and other nascent categories that, though tiny today, hint at entirely new classes of investible cash flows.

Add that up and the total amount of potentially assetizable assets outside of public markets comes in at $510 trillion—twice the size of public equity and bond markets combined.

Now to be clear: we are well aware that all of this value will, or should, turn into tradeable paper. Many assets will remain privately held, and not every loan, data stream, or music catalog needs to become a financial product. The numbers in this chapter are meant to be rough, order of magnitude estimates.

Yet these numbers are also tantalizing. Let's say that, for the sake of argument, over time 50% of these asset pools ultimately become accessible in investible form—tokenized, securitized, or wrapped in liquid vehicles. That would amount to some $255 trillion of additional assets entering portfolios.

That's quite a thought.

NOTES

1. Savills (2025). *How Much Is Global Real Estate Worth?* Available at: https://impacts.savills.com/market-trends/how-much-is-global-real-estate-worth.html (accessed 30 November 2025).
2. Nareit (2025). *Global Real Estate Investment: Opportunities & Insights*. Available at: https://www.reit.com/investing/global-real-estate-investment (accessed 30 November 2025).
3. ANREV, INREV and NCREIF (2025). *Fund Manager Survey 2025*. Available at: https://www.anrev.org/en/news/details/517/ (accessed 30 November 2025).
4. OECD (2025). *OECD Corporate Governance Factbook 2025*. Available at: https://www.oecd.org/en/publications/oecd-corporate-governance-factbook-2025_f4f43735-en.html (accessed 30 November 2025).

5. JoinGenius (2025). *How Many Companies Are There? New 2025 Statistics.* Available at: https://joingenius.com/statistics/how-many-companies-are-there/ (accessed 30 November 2025).

6. Scientific Infra & Private Assets (SIPA) (2024). *Private Equities Universe Report.* Available at: https://sipametrics.com/product/private-equities-universe-report/ (accessed 30 November 2025).

7. Finstock Capital (2025). *Bridging the Gap: The Evolving Landscape of UK SME Lending.* Available at: https://www.finstockcapital.com/new-blog/2025/4/28/bridging-the-gap-the-evolving-landscape-of-uk-sme-lending (accessed 30 November 2025).

8. McKinsey & Company (2024). *The Next Era of Private Credit.* Available at: https://www.mckinsey.com/industries/private-capital/our-insights/the-next-era-of-private-credit (accessed 30 November 2025).

9. PwC (2025). *Private Credit: Rewiring Credit in Capital Markets.* Available at: https://www.pwc.com/us/en/industries/financial-services/library/private-credit.html (accessed 13 January 2026).

10. Global Infrastructure Hub (2017). *Global Infrastructure Outlook.* Available at: https://outlook.gihub.org/ (accessed 30 November 2025).

11. CoinGecko (2025). *Cryptocurrency Market Charts.* Available at: https://www.coingecko.com/en/charts (accessed 30 November 2025).

12. Saklakov, A. (2025). *Global Crypto and Tokenised Asset Markets in 2030–2035: Base-Case Projections.* Available at: https://www.saklakov.com/blog/global-crypto-and-tokenised-asset-markets-in-2030-2035-base-case-projections (accessed 30 November 2025).

13. Deloitte (2023). *Art & Finance Report.* Available at: https://www.deloitte.com/ch/en/services/deloitte-private/research/art-and-finance-report.html (accessed 30 November 2025).

14. Gasaway, M., Eisman, D. and Bainou, B. (2025). *The resurgence of music securitization: Issuer and investor appeal in the data-driven era.* Reuters Legal News/Skadden, Arps, Slate, Meagher & Flom LLP. Available at: https://www.skadden.com/-/media/files/publications/2025/07/the_resurgence_of_music_securitization_issuer_and_investor_appeal_in_the_data_driven_era.pdf (accessed 30 November 2025).

15. Apollo Global Management (2025). *Concord: Largest-Ever Music ABS Transaction.* Available at: https://www.apollo.com/wealth/insights-news/insights/2025/01/apollo-leads-largest-ever-music-abs-transaction-for-concord (accessed 30 November 2025).

16. Khatri, U. (2024). *Polymarket's Huge Year: $9 Billion in Volume and 314,000 Active Traders Redefine Prediction Markets*. The Block. Available at: https://www.the block.co/post/333050/polymarkets-huge-year-9-billion-in-volume-and-314000-active-traders-redefine-prediction-markets (accessed 30 November 2025).

17. Grand View Research (2024). *Sports Betting Market Size, Share & Trends Report, 2024–2030*. Available at: https://www.grandviewresearch.com/industry-analysis/sports-betting-market-report (accessed 30 November 2025).

The vast majority of value sits outside public markets

We focus so much on the stock market that we forget it represents only a sliver of the global economy. The "untapped" world—private companies, real estate, infrastructure, and passion assets—dwarfs the listed world. Assetization is the key to turning tens of trillions of dollars of dormant value into active, investible capital.

Chapter Summary

- Public markets represent a shrinking percentage of global economic activity.
- Real Estate (~$393T): The world's largest asset class remains mostly illiquid.
- Private Companies (~$60T): Vast corporate value sits outside the reach of average investors.
- Private Credit (~$30T): Non-bank lending is filling the gap left by traditional banks.
- Infrastructure ($15T): A massive global funding gap requires private capital participation.
- Digital Assets (~$10T): A nascent market projected to reach vast scale as institutional adoption matures.
- Passion Assets (~$2T): Art and collectibles represent trillions of "storage wealth" earning zero yield.
- That's a total addressable market of $510 trillion. If half of that is assetized over time, it would represent $255 trillion of new investment opportunities.

"Assetization is about rethinking what qualifies as an asset and unlocking 'hidden' value. The magic happens when technology is deployed at the service of an increasingly participatory economy."

Dr. Efi Pylarinou, Global Fintech & Tech Influencer

"Assetization offers a new way to structure investment opportunities and broaden access — but doing so requires trust, transparency and institutional-grade processes."

Marc Blunier, Co-Head of Market Switzerland, Julius Bär

CHAPTER EIGHT

ASSETIZATION AND THE HISTORY OF FINANCE

Throughout this book, we've made our case for assetization based on various market, technological, and other forces. We also think that it's part of a much larger pattern.

If you look at the history of finance, you'll see that most innovation has been about increasing access, reducing friction, and expanding participation. From the invention of money to the rise of blockchain, each breakthrough has made finance more democratic—available to more people, cheaper to use, easier to understand.

Since assetization follows this mega-trend of democratization, we thought it would make sense to include a short history. In this chapter we trace the evolution of financial products from the early days to the present, with particular attention to securitization (since assetization grew directly from our attempts to make securitization easier and more accessible) and to the role of technology in breaking down barriers.

FINANCIAL PRODUCTS DEMOCRATIZE OVER TIME

If you want to find the origin moment in the democratization of finance, most historians would point to the invention of money itself. This seemingly simple innovation—replacing direct bartering with standardized units of value—fundamentally reduced the friction inherent in commerce. Money created a universal medium of exchange that made transactions faster, more flexible, and accessible to far more people.

The real leap came with paper currency. Notes offered dramatic advantages in scalability and convenience—easier to produce in quantity, lighter to transport, simpler to authenticate than metal coins. Paper money was, in essence, the first great "containerization" of financial value. This innovation made it feasible to create enough circulating currency for entire populations rather than just wealthy elites.

The creation of legal entities offering limited liability marked the birth of financial engineering in earnest. By capping the downside risk of business ventures, limited liability enabled ordinary people to start businesses without risking their entire personal wealth. This dramatically lowered the barriers to commercial activity.

The early seventeenth century brought us joint-stock companies, perhaps the first true democratization of investment opportunity. Before this, only the exceptionally wealthy could finance large-scale trade ventures. Joint-stock structures allowed capital to be pooled from multiple investors of modest means, enabling ordinary merchants and professionals to participate in ventures they could never have afforded individually.

Formal stock exchanges, beginning with institutions like the New York Stock Exchange in the nineteenth century, created standardized, transparent markets where ownership stakes could be traded efficiently. However, access remained distinctly "gated"—limited to those who could afford professional brokers and meet minimum investment thresholds.

The 1920s witnessed what many consider the most pivotal moment in financial democratization: the creation of mutual funds. These vehicles allowed ordinary people to pool their money and gain access to professionally managed, diversified portfolios—something previously available only to wealthy individuals with substantial capital. For the first time, small investors could participate in stock market growth without needing the capital to build diversified portfolios themselves.

The post-World War II boom accelerated financial democratization dramatically through employer-sponsored retirement plans. The introduction of 401(k)s and IRAs in the United States fundamentally changed the relationship between ordinary Americans and financial markets. These programs didn't just make investing accessible—they made it systematic and often automatic through payroll deductions, bringing millions of middle-class households into the markets as regular, long-term investors.

The 1970s and 1980s saw discount brokerage firms fundamentally disrupt the traditional, high-cost brokerage model. By offering significantly lower trading costs, these firms made active investing affordable for average individuals with modest portfolios.

The World Wide Web revolution of the 1990s transformed finance as profoundly as any single innovation. Online trading platforms didn't just make markets more accessible—they democratized information itself. Individual investors could suddenly access real-time market data, research reports, and analytical tools that had previously been the exclusive domain of professional traders.

Exchange-traded funds, introduced in the 1990s, represented another breakthrough. Like mutual funds, ETFs offered diversification and professional management at reasonable costs. But by trading on exchanges like individual stocks, they provided much greater flexibility. The proliferation of ETFs enabled retail investors to implement institutional-quality investment strategies.

The 2010s brought robo-advisors, which democratized not just market access but also professional-quality financial advice. By using algorithms to automate investment planning and portfolio management, these platforms made personalized financial guidance available at a fraction of the cost of traditional human advisors.

Perhaps one of the most profound democratizing forces has been the explosion of accessible financial education. Where investment knowledge was once closely guarded, today's digital platforms have made learning about sophisticated financial concepts available to anyone with an internet connection. YouTube channels, podcasts, and free online courses have transformed financial literacy from an elite privilege into a widely accessible skill.

The emergence of blockchain technology and decentralized finance represents another radical democratization of financial services. Public blockchains operate on community consensus rather than centralized authority. DeFi platforms allow anyone with an internet connection to access lending, borrowing, and trading services without requiring a relationship with a traditional bank or brokerage.

Stablecoins represent a fundamental innovation in monetary technology—creating programmable money that operates across borders without traditional banking infrastructure. For millions in countries with unstable currencies or limited banking infrastructure, stablecoins provide access to stable value and efficient payment systems.

Among the most profound recent developments is the embedding of financial services directly into other applications. Ride-sharing apps include integrated payments, e-commerce platforms offer instant credit, and social media applications enable direct peer-to-peer transactions. By removing the friction of accessing financial services altogether, embedded finance represents the ultimate democratization—making finance so seamless that it becomes a natural part of everyday digital life.

A SHORT HISTORY OF SECURITIZATION

Since assetization grew out of our attempts to make securitization easier and more democratic, a short history of this practice makes sense here as well.

In the financial industry, "securitization" refers to pooling assets into investible financial products or "securities." The basic idea is simple: take illiquid assets that generate returns—like mortgages or loan payments—package them together, and sell shares in that package to investors.

Modern securitization began in the United States in the 1970s with mortgage-backed securities. Government entities and banks started aggregating residential mortgages into packages that were then securitized and sold to investors. This was actively encouraged by the US government as a solution to a housing crisis. The logic was elegant: if mortgage-backed securities could attract investor capital, then mortgage originators could sell their loans and use the money to make new mortgages.

The idea worked very well. Financial institutions quickly saw the broader potential and began applying the same principles to automobile loans, credit card debt, student loans, and equipment financing. The pattern was consistent: securitization created liquidity where none had existed before, lowering costs and expanding access.

The financial crisis of 2008 severely damaged securitization's reputation, but the problems came from poor execution rather than flaws in the concept itself. Rapid growth had led to declining standards and excessive risk-taking among mortgage providers. These issues reflected poor implementation and inadequate oversight, not problems with securitization itself.

Beyond traditional financial assets, securitization has proven adaptable to alternative asset classes, including collectibles, fine art, wine, and commodities. Any asset that generates predictable cash flows or appreciates in value can potentially be securitized. The basic principles of pooling and standardization can unlock value in virtually any asset class.

What makes securitization a truly democratizing force is its ability to increase access and broaden investment opportunities. By transforming illiquid assets into tradable securities, the process makes a much wider variety of investments available to a broader range of investors. The pooling mechanism also reduces risk—instead of owning a single mortgage or loan, investors hold fractional interests in hundreds or thousands of similar assets.

THE ROLE OF TECHNOLOGY

It's impossible to underestimate the importance of technology in modern financial services in general, as well as its role in helping to democratize access to these services. Without digitalization, we couldn't have a global financial system. Technology makes it possible to send money around the world, to build global financial markets, to get instant access to information, to do our daily banking from the comfort of our homes, and so on. There is hardly any area of our financial system that doesn't rely on technology to some degree.

Technology has also greatly democratized access to financial services. Thanks to modern communications anyone in the world with an internet connection can make at least some use of the global financial system.

And the trend is to continually make things easier, for example by going from ebanking at home to ebanking "on the go" via a mobile device.

Finally, technology has enabled the growth of large online platforms and led to what is often referred to as the "platform economy."

The business case of online platforms often revolves around the removal of a number of middlemen in favor of the platform that acts as a single, all-encompassing middleman or aggregator of products and services. This has led to some interesting new business models.

The classic example is Uber, the world's largest taxi company even though it does not own any taxis.

Platforms like these have a democratizing function in the sense that they allow more people to create, connect, and/or transact directly. The net effect is almost always less friction, greater access, and more opportunity. In many cases, they also mean lower prices for consumers. Yet this need not always be the case. Thanks to surge pricing, taking an Uber can at times cost more than a regular taxi. But people are willing to pay because of the ease of use. The removal of friction can be very valuable to people. Using technology to build assetization platforms will have a similar effect. Making this readily available via a platform will increase access to the benefits of assetization and reduce friction in the same way other platforms do.

The development of robust Application Programming Interfaces (APIs) created another significant reduction in friction. Before APIs, integrating different financial systems required custom programming and expensive technical work. Modern financial APIs changed this completely. Services like Plaid made it possible to connect to thousands of banks with just a few lines of code. This dramatically reduced the time and capital required to launch new financial services.

Finally, as we have seen, AI is transforming and democratizing financial services by eliminating friction across the value chain, automating complex tasks like portfolio management and compliance that once required expensive specialists, widening access to sophisticated tools and products, and beginning to erode the traditional barriers between institutions and individuals, setting the stage for the most profound democratization of finance since the invention of money.

EVERYTHING BUILDS ON EVERYTHING ELSE

What's remarkable about this technological progression is how each wave has accelerated the next. Computing made electronic trading possible. Electronic trading created demand for better information systems. The internet enabled mobile platforms. Mobile platforms created demand for API integration. APIs enabled AI personalization.

Each technological solution to financial friction has also revealed new opportunities to reduce barriers that weren't obvious before. The internet didn't just make existing financial information cheaper—it made entirely new forms of financial education and community possible. Mobile didn't just make existing services more convenient—it enabled financial inclusion in markets where traditional infrastructure had never existed.

This technological momentum continues to accelerate. Cloud computing makes sophisticated financial infrastructure available without major capital investments. Machine learning makes personalization scalable. Blockchain makes global financial services possible without traditional regulatory frameworks.

We keep seeing the same pattern: technology spots friction, eliminates it, and in doing so, opens access to groups who were previously shut out. This is what is happening with assetization too.

History favors open markets

This revolution is not a temporary trend; it is the continuation of a centuries-long arc. From the invention of paper money to the joint-stock company to the ETF, the history of finance is a history of technology reducing friction and expanding access. Assetization is simply the latest, inevitable chapter in this story.

Chapter Summary

- Financial history follows a consistent pattern: increasing access and reducing friction.

- Paper Money: The first innovation that made value scalable and easier to transport.

- Joint-Stock Companies: Allowed ordinary people to pool capital for the first time.

- Mutual Funds: Democratized professional management, once a privilege of the wealthy.

- ETFs: Gave retail investors the flexibility and strategies of institutions.

- Technology: From mainframes to the internet, every leap lowered costs and removed barriers.

- The Pattern: Technology spots friction, eliminates it, and opens the door to new participants.

- Assetization is just the latest iteration of this unstoppable historical force.

"Assetization is one of the biggest megatrends currently in finance and might be the most relevant use case of the convergence of finance and technology."

Marc P. Bernegger, Founding Partner, Maximon; Chairman, Longevity Investors

"Assetization represents one of the last great frontiers of investing. As this book makes clear, it is an important idea whose time has come."

Rainer-Marc Frey, Chairman SO Holding AG

CHAPTER NINE

INVEST IN YOUR BELIEFS

W hen Patrick and Philippe stood in that Zurich nightclub in 2018, about to announce their new company, they thought they were solving a technical problem: making nonbankable assets bankable. In reality, they were stepping into a much broader transformation already reshaping the investment industry.

We have called that shift assetization and traced it through three waves of democratization, following Ada the investor, Barbara the independent advisor, and Clark the institutional wealth manager to make the story tangible.

In this final chapter, we bring it back to what this means for each of them—and for you. We address investors, advisors, and wealth managers in turn, moving from the framework we've built to the practical choices each group faces.

FOR ADAS: INVEST IN YOUR BELIEFS

If you are an investor like Ada, assetization changes the basic question your portfolio answers. Instead of "What's on the shelf?" the question becomes "What do I actually believe about the world, and how do I express that through what I own?"

For too long, you were constrained by an artificial definition of "investible." You were told that listed equities and bonds, plus a few mutual funds and ETFs, more or less were "the market," and you adjusted your expectations accordingly. Meanwhile, your portfolio became increasingly concentrated in public markets, more correlated across holdings, and less genuinely diversified, even as huge pools of value in private markets, real assets, and alternative strategies remained inaccessible.

That boundary is now moving. As we've tried to show, trillions of dollars in previously unreachable assets—from private equity and private credit to infrastructure, real estate, and passion assets—are becoming accessible through new wrappers and platforms. This is not just about chasing higher returns; it is about building portfolios with exposure to different drivers of value so that all your assets do not move in lockstep.

Real diversification means combining assets and strategies that respond differently to economic conditions and reflect multiple views of the future. It gives you portfolios that can weather shocks, capture opportunities others cannot reach, and align more closely with the real economy rather than just the small slice represented by public markets.

Most importantly, your portfolio can now be uniquely yours. It can reflect what you know, what you care about, and where you see opportunity, instead of being a slightly customized version of the same model everyone else owns. For years, the products, tools, and economics made this kind of personalization unrealistic. Now they do not.

In a world where information and access sit in your pocket, your edge is your perspective. Staying curious, questioning standard narratives, and forming your own convictions matters more than ever, because you increasingly have the ability to act on those convictions across a much broader universe of assets.

This does not mean chasing every trend or treating speculation as a strategy. It means refusing to accept that the only valid investments are the ones someone else found convenient to manufacture. If you see a sector, theme, or shift in the economy that you believe in, you are entitled to ask: "How do I invest in this—and why not?"

The infrastructure is being built. The tools are coming online. The industry is moving in this direction. Your task is to articulate what you believe and demand that your advisors, platforms, and institutions help you express it.

FOR BARBARAS: BUILD WHAT YOU BELIEVE

If you are an independent advisor like Barbara, you have spent years watching your world compress. Clients have more information, more low-cost options, and less patience for standardized portfolios that look interchangeable from one firm to the next, while much of the value you create is hidden behind the brands of the products you distribute.

Assetization offers you a way to reverse that dynamic. Instead of being a conduit for other people's funds, you can become the architect of solutions that carry your fingerprint and reflect what you believe your clients truly need. You can design products and vehicles that embody your research, your judgment, and your understanding of your clients' goals—and have clients associate those solutions directly with you.

This does not require abandoning core building blocks. Public-market funds, model portfolios, and established managers still have their place.

The difference is that you can now add a layer of customization and product creation on top of them—expressing specific themes, risk preferences, time horizons, and constraints that off-the-shelf products cannot capture on their own.

Modern creation platforms, standardized legal containers, and outsourced infrastructure mean you no longer need a bank's balance sheet or a large asset manager's operations to bring a product to life. You need clarity about your clients, a willingness to experiment within robust governance, and the conviction to step out from behind other brands.

Advisors who move first will define the new expectations. They will build track records as creators, not just curators; they will attract clients who want more than generic allocation; and they will build businesses that are differentiated, defensible, and harder to undercut on price alone.

You already listen to your clients, see where standard products fall short, and spot opportunities the industry overlooks. Assetization finally gives you tools to act on those professional beliefs—to build, not just to select. The opportunity is real, but it is not permanent. As these tools become mainstream, what is distinctive today will become tomorrow's minimum.

FOR CLARKS: BACK THE FUTURE YOU BELIEVE IN

If you are an institutional wealth manager like Clark, your challenge is different. You operate within layers of process, legacy systems, and justifiable risk and compliance constraints, and you cannot simply launch products because a client asked for them yesterday.

At the same time, you can see the ground shifting. Younger clients are experimenting outside your walls, moving assets to platforms you do not control, and demanding exposures your current toolkit cannot deliver. Internal innovation cycles that once felt prudently conservative now risk irrelevance.

Assetization gives you language and leverage to advocate for change from within, based on your belief that the institution must evolve to remain relevant. You can frame new creation tools and alternative-access platforms not as threats to governance, but as structured, compliant ways to meet real client demand before it migrates elsewhere.

Pilot programs, limited mandates, and clearly defined suitability rules let you introduce these capabilities in a controlled way, measure their impact, and build institutional comfort step by step. Once such pathways exist, you can finally say "yes—and here is the approved way we can do it" instead of apologizing for the limits of legacy menus.

You will never have the flexibility of an independent advisor. But you have scale, trust, and regulatory infrastructure that many clients still value deeply. By adopting assetization tools and integrating them into your operating model, you can add agility to that stability and keep more of the experimentation—and the assets—inside your ecosystem rather than watching them drift away.

You may not lead the revolution. But you can decide to back the future you believe is coming and make sure your institution participates in it and survives it.

IN SUM

To recap: The core argument of this book is that the investment industry is undergoing a structural shift. For the first time, the tools of financial product creation are moving beyond a handful of large institutions to the broader buy side. Access to previously unreachable assets is expanding, and the line between those who select investments and those who manufacture them is starting to blur.

This matters because it unlocks capital. Trillions of dollars in real assets—private companies, infrastructure, real estate, alternative strategies, and more—can increasingly be turned into investible instruments, allowing capital to flow toward a much wider set of needs and opportunities than the traditional system ever supported.

It matters because it enables genuine diversification. Investors can build portfolios that reflect the true breadth of the economy and of human activity, rather than the narrow subset represented by listed securities.

And it matters because it shifts power. Independent advisors can compete on creation, not just distribution. Institutional wealth managers can modernize without abandoning oversight. Individual investors can express convictions instead of simply accepting what is offered. The people closest to real needs—from financing small businesses to funding infrastructure to structuring bespoke solutions—can now build the products to meet them.

The investment world is more open and accessible than it has ever been. What happens next depends on who chooses to act: on whether investors insist on portfolios that reflect their beliefs, whether advisors build what they believe their clients need, and whether institutions modernize around the future they believe is coming.

The revolution belongs to those who act

The infrastructure is changing, barriers are falling, and the transition is underway. The distinction between those who select investments and those who create them is blurring fast. For investors, advisors, and institutions alike, the risk is no longer "trying something new"—the risk is standing still while the world moves on.

Chapter Summary

- The investment world is more open and accessible than it has ever been.

- For Investors: You now have the power to invest in your beliefs—not just in an ESG sense, but in your true convictions.

- Don't settle for a standardized shelf; build a portfolio that reflects your unique view of the world.

- For Advisors: Stop being a middleman. Become an architect who builds solutions, not just a curator who picks them.

- For Institutions: Bring innovation inside. Use partnerships to offer the agility clients demand without losing control.

- The distinction between the "buy side" and the "sell side" is disappearing.

- Trillions of dollars in real value are becoming investible, allowing for true diversification.

- The tools are ready. The question isn't if assetization will happen, but who will seize the opportunity.

PART II

ASSET RUSH— TALES FROM THE ASSETIZATION FRONTIER

T his Part lets you hear directly from people making assetization happen.

Over the past few years, we've spoken with innovators across the investment frontier—platform builders, asset managers, wealth advisors, academics, entrepreneurs, custody specialists, and industry veterans. They're working in different corners of finance, tackling different problems, but all wrestling with similar questions about what becomes possible when the barriers to accessing and creating financial products begin to fall.

These conversations originally appeared on our podcast, *The Assetizer*, or were conducted specifically for this book. We've edited them for clarity and flow, but the substance is theirs. What follows are their insights, their approaches, their predictions, and sometimes their cautions.

Several themes emerge across these conversations, even though the speakers come from vastly different contexts.

Infrastructure is foundational. Whether it's Nisha Surendran explaining how Citi builds custody for digital assets, Professor Lisa Wilson describing the two-year process of making carbon credits genuinely investible, or Mark Arasaratnam detailing how GenTwo Digital solves institutional crypto's access problem, the work of assetization isn't just about wrapping assets in certificates. It's about building the rails—the custody solutions, the compliance frameworks, the trust layers—that make new asset classes actually bankable.

Practical constraints shape everything. Myriam Oualha Deblanc discusses the cultural and psychological dimensions of portfolio construction. Patrick Michaels explains why active management still wins in mining and commodities. Pascal Schneidinger details the off-market sourcing and due diligence required to make fine art investible. These aren't people building in a vacuum. They're solving real problems for real clients, constrained by regulation, market structure, human behavior, and the simple fact that most innovations require an entire ecosystem to work.

Academic perspective matters too. Professor Kean Birch traces how assetization became a scholarly field, exploring intellectual property, natural capital, and data as assets. Professor Wilson brings rigorous climate science to bear on carbon markets. Pier-Luc Nappert studies what happens when minor league baseball players voluntarily turn themselves into investible assets. The academic lens reveals patterns and implications that practitioners, focused on building, might miss.

Technology enables but doesn't determine outcomes. Joe Lubin and Joseph Chalom discuss Ethereum as infrastructure for settlement and programmability. Lucas Ereth explains why the power of assetization comes from network effects in the traditional banking system, not just blockchain innovation. The conversation isn't "crypto versus traditional"—it's about how different infrastructures solve different problems and, increasingly, how they interoperate.

Personalization becomes possible at scale. Pete Casella frames assetization as enabling true investment personalization—portfolios that reflect individual beliefs rather than mass-market templates. This isn't just theory. Across these conversations, you see it in practice: uranium exposure for institutional investors, carbon credits for impact allocators, structured products for wealth managers, art portfolios for qualified investors. The common thread is that things that were once accessible only to insiders or institutions are becoming available in formats that work within existing financial infrastructure.

The opportunity is vast but the work is detailed. Everyone mentions the trillions—trillions in private markets, trillions in alternative assets, trillions in previously inaccessible value. But nobody suggests this happens automatically. Every conversation reveals painstaking work: sourcing assets off-market, building digital custody solutions, creating ex-ante rating systems, negotiating with regulators, educating investors, solving for the temporal mismatch between 24/7 blockchain rails and traditional settlement windows.

What you won't find here is a unified vision of what assetization becomes. These speakers don't all agree on timelines, on which asset classes matter most, on whether retail or institutional adoption leads, on how much infrastructure needs to change before things really scale. That's fine.

Assetization is still taking shape. The people building it are figuring it out as they go.

What they do share is a recognition that something fundamental is shifting. The barriers to product creation are falling. The infrastructure is disaggregating. Access is broadening. And the investment universe—what counts as investible, who gets to create products, who gets to participate—is expanding in ways that looked impossible a decade ago.

These are the voices from that frontier.

A note on terminology: Several conversations in this section refer to "actively managed certificates" or AMCs. An Actively Managed Certificate (AMC) is a flexible investment product that allows asset managers, advisors, and institutions to package and implement an investment strategy without the complexity of setting up a fund. Think of it as a wrapper: inside, one or more underlying assets, equities, bonds, alternatives, or digital assets, that are actively managed in real time. Once issued, capital raised from investors flows directly into the portfolio, with strategy managers free to adjust holdings within a defined investment universe. Unlike traditional structured products with fixed compositions, AMCs are dynamic. The portfolio can be adapted to market shifts, investor preferences, or new opportunities, all while remaining fully bankable. They represent one approach to customizing the interior of the securitization container discussed in Part I.

THE CHANGING FACE OF ASSET MANAGEMENT: MYRIAM OUALHA DEBLANC

This interview explores how cultural background, generational differences, and psychological factors shape investment decisions—dimensions that automation and standardization often overlook. The discussion of why advisors must combine human judgment with technology speaks directly to whether assetization empowers advisory practices or threatens to replace them.

M yriam Oualha Deblanc describes herself as "the hippie of structured products and derivatives," referring to her mission to bring a more artistic, intuitive approach to what is a highly technical field. After working at Commerzbank and Royal Bank of Canada, she founded her own firm, ProFin Partners, in 2009 following the Lehman crisis. The company was based on a realization that remains central today: financial services isn't just about pricing. It's also about expertise, advisory, and understanding human needs.

ProFin started by restructuring portfolios of clients who'd invested in bad products. That remains the DNA. "We try to understand the needs of the clients," Myriam explains. "Most of the time they don't know what they need. They follow trends. So my team challenges them to understand what they want to achieve, what they don't want, and from there we create an investment idea."

When Myriam examines a troubled portfolio, she starts with diagnosis rather than prescription. "When I see a portfolio, I try to understand how did we end up in that situation? Usually a client will say they're not happy with their portfolio without knowing why. They look at the performance, but I think it's deeper than that. We analyze and try to understand: is there a pattern? Is the client more into technology? More into yield and capital protection? In most cases, the client invested because of bad advice or how the solution was packaged."

Once the pattern becomes clear, difficult conversations follow. "We realize that some products will not perform any better. So we cut the losses. This is where you have to be a bit of a psychologist, because cutting losses is not easy. But we start from a healthier portfolio."

Growing up in Tunisia with a European mother and Tunisian father, then working across the Middle East and Asia, gave Myriam a practical education in how culture shapes investment decisions.

"I look at life and investment the same way," she says. "How you live, you will invest. How you consume, you will invest. In countries where there's been war or uncertainty, they look at duration differently than a European investor. One year for some Middle Eastern investors is too long, whereas for Europeans it's too short. Some will say a return of 6% is too high. Middle Eastern investors might say it's too low—they want double digits. That's related to the ecosystem they grew up in, the uncertainty, whether they trust the country they're in, whether they want liquidity or capital preservation. Religion has an impact too. Catholics invest differently than Protestants, for instance."

The structured products industry has evolved considerably over Myriam's career, and not always for the better. "When I started, you had very few products, very few payouts and payoffs. You were focused on the fundamentals. What is my return? What is my risk? You were talking about a few things, and it made more sense."

Then automation arrived. "FinTech changed things. Before, when someone said, 'I want a risk adjusted investment,' you had to go on Bloomberg and check—okay, Nvidia's low point was this level, so I'll build a product around that support. There was more thinking than today. Today you go on the machine and just do pricing—100, 200, 300 pricings. Of course you have more options, but you tend not to think too much. So there's quantity over quality."

The post-Lehman generation grew up differently. "The new generation of providers grew up in a low-rate, low-volatility environment. They know funky products and sophisticated structures, but not the plain vanilla basics."

What clients want has shifted as well. "Before it was 'What is the best product?' What are your convictions? What do you think about the markets?' Now it's 'What is the best pricing? What is my optimized return versus my fee versus my cost?' Optimization is an obsession today. Before, we'd have discussions about one product a month at higher volume. Today, clients want products every day but less volume. There's an obsession, an adrenaline rush, fed by the machine, the automation, WhatsApp. You can converse with clients in a very easy way."

The most significant shift, though, is generational. Most of Myriam's clients are 55–60 years old, with wealthy families and next generation heirs. COVID accelerated a disconnect that was already forming.

"The big change happened with COVID. A lot of private banks could not sustain the demand of the next generation. They wanted to do Bitcoin, futures, the VIX, play volatility. This next generation started saying, 'No, dad, mom, I don't want a private banker. I don't want a family office. By the time I tell them what I want to do, everything has changed. They don't understand private equity, Bitcoin, art, leverage. They want me to sign bloody papers and forms. I'll go on Interactive Brokers or just do it myself.'"

The pattern is consistent. "The next generation is changing. There's little commitment, little time. They want it now, quick, at a good price, and then they move on to the next investment and the next and the next. It's a different way of looking at things."

The appetite for alternative investments and private markets is growing, but barriers remain. "There will be more and more appetite for unlisted or private markets. There's an appetite for new things—people want to be trendy but do it quickly. The main issue for the next generation is they don't own the wealth yet. Maybe a pocket of it, a small portion. The obstacle is whoever is guarding the wealth, whether it's a trustee or private banker, because the old generation is not really interested in new investments unless it's their own business."

If a wealthy family wants to raise finance for their business, private credit or private equity makes sense. "But when a family member wants to invest in fine art or tokenization of art, whatever it is, the family board might not support the idea. The CIO or family office see it as a danger or risk." Getting to this generation requires patience. "It's a matter of time and education."

With the next generation wanting to trade on platforms and do everything themselves, automation and AI becoming ubiquitous, an obvious question emerges: do we still need advisors at all?

"I think we need advisors in the future," she says. "The advisory element goes with creativity. But now with technology and AI, a lot of people will hide behind the machine. 'Oh, it's not me, it's the machine. It's the client who logged in and pressed the wrong button.'"

She sees this dynamic with her own team. "I use FinTech in the company, and I see my guys—I call them the youngsters—they're on the machine. It's like adrenaline. Like a little video game. But I'm trying to tell them, this machine or AI or FinTech is here to save you time so you can use your brain for other things. But it's difficult for them because they feel like, 'Why do I have to do my homework? Mom, the machine is doing it. Why do I have to go to school? I can make money today.'"

Myriam has little patience for asset managers without real added value. "When I say no added value, I mean in terms of quality of service, quality of ideas, quality versus quantity. Those asset managers shouldn't even exist. They're just here to take fees and not really care, especially when products go wrong."

But there's a place for those who bring genuine expertise. "Asset managers or advisors who are aligned with their clients and say, 'Things can go wrong, can go right. Nothing's perfect'—those asset managers will survive. There will be an evolution. They'll look at other asset classes, be more open. They'll take on the younger generation and teach them the know-how they've had in the conventional way."

Her formula is straightforward: "I always say to my team and my clients, you have to combine artificial with human intelligence. The artificial intelligence is here to do the things you don't have time for, but then it gives you time to think. It's not always easy, but I believe you have to have both."

FINTECH EXISTS TO MAKE THINGS EASIER FOR PEOPLE: PETE CASELLA

This interview examines how reducing friction in financial services has historically driven democratization. The discussion traces the pattern from mutual funds through ETFs to assetization, arguing that infrastructure innovations matter most when they remove barriers rather than simply reduce costs. The concept of "investment personalization" connects directly to what becomes possible when product creation tools become accessible.

Pete Casella is co-founder and CEO of Stack Asset Management. He was founding partner of Point72 Ventures and before that spent over a decade in fintech venture capital at JPMorgan Chase and Credit

Suisse. We talked to him about assetization, the role of fintech in financial innovation, and what happens when every asset class becomes accessible.

Casella has a foundational view about financial services that shapes how he sees everything else. "Financial services are not an end in themselves, they are a means, a lubricant," he says. "They exist to make things easier. All progress or innovation in financial services is to this end. That's an important basic concept, though people in our industry sometimes lose sight of it."

He pushes the point further. "The truth is, nobody shops for financial products as such. You don't shop for an auto loan. You shop for a car, and you need an auto loan to buy the car. You don't shop for a mortgage. You shop for a house, and then you need a mortgage to buy the house. And so on."

This isn't just philosophy. For Casella, it's the lens through which to understand what fintech actually does. "Everything financial services companies do is simply to allow something to happen more efficiently or more effectively than a person could do on their own. The role of fintech is to apply technology and new thinking into this process of continually making things easier, to accelerate it, and to bring it to more people."

The examples are everywhere. Take mortgages. "In the past, if you wanted to get a mortgage, you would have had to go to a bank and put in an application and go through a manual underwriting process and then at the end of it, you would have been presented with a whole bunch of paper documents," Casella explains. "Today the mortgage industry is trying to make the application process easier. They're trying to make the underwriting process easier. And that can only be done with technology and new thinking."

Same thing with auto loans. "The auto industry is trying to push the auto loan process closer and closer into the dealership, so that when you're there looking at the car you can also get the loan and leave the dealership with the car. Technology plays a role here too."

But it's in the investment industry where Casella sees the clearest pattern and where the groundwork for assetization was laid. He points to the shift from mutual funds to ETFs as the key precedent.

"Since the 1920s, the primary way that investors got access to index-based exposures, so portfolios of stocks or portfolios of bonds, was largely through mutual funds. But they weren't easy to run or use. You had to send your money to the mutual fund manager. The mutual fund manager had to take that cash and go into the market and buy stocks and put them into the portfolio. And when you needed to get your money out, you had to tell them and the fund needed to sell those stocks to free up the cash. And that had tax implications. And so on. It was a high-friction, high-fee product."

Then came the innovation. "And then along came exchange traded funds, which gave you the same exposure by creating a tracker against an index. And that allowed for a number of efficiencies and benefits, making for a lower friction, lower fee product."

The result was dramatic. "When that happened, a ton of assets flowed out of the mutual fund world and into the ETF world. It expanded the universe of who was able to invest in the product. That's exactly the evolution we have been talking about."

But ETFs had limits. "They were a great innovation," Casella says, "but they struggle with a number of different things, like active management or illiquid asset classes."

The workarounds weren't satisfactory. "For a long period of time, the only way to get access to these was either through a hedge fund type structure or via active management, in which case, it looks just like a mutual fund. There is the same friction. Another alternative was through a structured product. But that tended to be bank issued, which meant you could get the product that you wanted, but you had to take counterparty credit risk. And we saw what happened for example with Credit Suisse and in many other cases recently."

This left a narrow investor base. "The end effect is that the only people that have been investing in alternative asset classes are ultra-high-net-worth individuals, qualified investors, institutions, or people who understand counterparty credit risk."

This is where Casella sees assetization fitting in. "What I believe assetization is all about, and what companies like GenTwo are solving, is the ability to provide that exposure without the counterparty credit risk of a banking institution. It's a vehicle that allows you to have exposure to esoteric, innovative, long-short, multi-asset class, illiquid type strategies in the same way that a hedge fund might, but without the hedge fund."

He's direct about what this means. "GenTwo is a perfect example of how technology and new thinking open things up. It allows people to get involved in the industry that weren't involved in the past. It allows asset managers to offer these types of products to customers that were historically unable to access them. And because it's technology enabled, it reduces the overall operating cost to launch a product, which should produce downward pressure on fees over the long term. That's really assetization in a nutshell."

Looking ahead, Casella sees this opening up something that hasn't really been possible before: genuine investment personalization. "No two investors are created equal," he says. "You and I may be substantially similar in terms of our age and our risk tolerance and our investable assets, but my portfolio should be a reflection of my beliefs. Obviously, there's some rules in there, of course. Like you should make sure you're abiding by some portfolio best practices around diversification and risk and things like that. But generally, the things that I believe in are very unique to me."

He takes the thought further. "My guess is if you were to look at every person in the world that has money to invest, if you were to really give them all the tools to express their viewpoints, there will be slight differences between every single person. What investors want, and what assetization gives them, is the ability to invest in their beliefs, whatever they are."

The constraint has been access. "Yet historically, based on the products that were available to invest in or that were easily accessible, people were constrained. It has not really been possible to express investment views in a truly personalized way. Only in a world where all asset classes and sub-asset classes are accessible in an easy way can you see a movement toward true investment personalization."

For asset managers, it's the flip side. "The precondition for investors being able to invest in anything that they believe in is that asset managers have the ability to create the products that they believe investors want. And if today they're constrained by their own balance sheet or their own credit rating or their own distribution channels, it's going to stifle the true creativity and product development that would satisfy investor interest."

He's clear-eyed about where things stand. "We're not at the stage yet where the end investors have true democratization. In order for that to happen, you need to assetize every asset class. Which means that professional investment managers need to identify all of the hardest to access asset classes and strategies and they need to find all the difficult things to do and use this product innovation to then do them and make them available to end investors who don't even know they need it yet."

The market size implications are substantial, but Casella frames it as fundamentally an access problem. "For the largest liquid asset classes like US stocks, there are a plethora of ways an investor can get access. They can buy stocks through any number of brokers, through advisors, through mutual funds, ETFs, etc. As the asset class becomes less liquid, or more speculative, the range of access vehicles decreases as does your ability to actually get access to the vehicles."

He gives concrete examples. "Think about fine art, that's the domain of art collectors. Unless you have significant capital and know exactly how to find masterworks, that's just not available to you. Or investing in private companies through a venture capital round. The only investors coming into a VC round are funds that are hand-selected by management. Very few are chosen, and most of these funds are only accessible to large institutional investors or people who have direct relationships with the management teams of the funds."

These aren't small categories. "These are massive asset classes with unique risk return characteristics, but the vast majority of investors do not have any of this exposure in their portfolios. As assetization enables more of these categories to become investible, they will become more accessible to a wider range of investors, and allocations will follow growing the overall capital coming from new funding sources."

And then there's what comes after the obvious use cases. Casella reaches for a technological analogy. "It's only a natural outcome. Once a technical innovation unlocks creativity, innovators will find ways to use it that were not even considered in the past. The iPhone paved the way for the AppStore, which enabled developers to build mobile applications. That spawned a vast ecosystem of new business models and industries that you couldn't have imagined when you first saw a touch screen phone that had the internet."

He applies this to assetization. "At first with assetization, the innovation will be obvious to the end user. It will be products that they know exist elsewhere but have just never been given the chance to access. But as innovators learn how to use financial technology to build new things, and they see that it is economically attractive to build things that people will buy, they will start experimenting. And those experiments will lead to a lot of flops but will also lead to things that nobody had ever considered. And the entire nature of investing will change as a result."

MAKING CARBON CREDITS INVESTIBLE: PROFESSOR LISA WILSON

This interview details the infrastructure requirements for making carbon credits institutionally investible. The two-year process illustrates what assetization demands beyond financial engineering: building custody solutions, establishing provenance systems, creating rating frameworks, and assembling the trust layer that transforms fragmented commodities into bankable asset classes.

Professor Lisa Wilson is a globally recognized business leader and academic in climate science and digital assets with an industry-based professorship from South Africa. Her career has spanned mining, healthcare, heavy construction, and now climate finance. She is a preeminent "ecosystem design thinker," which is someone who solves difficult problems by understanding how all the component parts of the challenge work together. As Wilson says, "If you're going to innovate, you have to innovate an entire ecosystem, not part of it."

This mindset shaped her greater than two-year project: Overcoming market obstructions to ensure capital flows with the volume and velocity required by making carbon credits an investible commodity at institutional scale.

The problem was clear. At COP28 in Dubai, Kristalina Georgieva, head of the IMF, made a statement that stuck with Wilson: we need "trillions of dollars to flow unobstructed from capital markets" into climate projects and decarbonization programs to deliver on climate and sustainability goals. The key word for Wilson was "unobstructed." The scale is staggering: $175 billion a year just for ocean-related climate work, while only $5–10 billion currently flows. The money exists in institutional capital markets—pension funds, asset managers, banks—but there are no tools allowing them to invest in climate projects without hitting regulatory or structural obstacles. "There are no financial tools that de-risk their mandates and allow them to invest into climate."

The challenge wasn't creating a new financial instrument—actively managed certificates have existed for years. The challenge was that carbon credits themselves weren't investible at the scale institutional investors required and didn't fit the usual mold for an AMC structure.

Professor Wilson asks you to imagine a scenario: "Let's just say that I have an investor that comes in with $500 million and we have to go out and curate those carbon assets from a myriad of projects—verified projects with all different attributes. We might have to go out to 30 to 40 different projects that have their assets sitting on different registries. It could be 20 to 30 individual registries around the world. And we'll have 14 to 15 different financial jurisdictions."

The fragmentation creates an immediate custody problem. "Carbon credits are produced using specific methodologies, and each methodology is tied to a particular registry. So, if I go out and I want to buy $500 million worth of assets, I've probably got 15 different registries, and different jurisdictions. It's almost like I'm saying, can you give me a shoebox full of receipts? And in that shoebox is my asset class of carbon credits."

But the real problem comes after purchase. "What happens is when those assets are bought, they then become orphaned from the registry. So, they've got to go somewhere. Where do I put those assets as an investment for somebody to invest into?"

Traditional financial infrastructure doesn't work. "Entities like our paying agent, they're very used to having gold because they can see gold go from one vault to another vault, and they're all regulated and secure. But how do I give the paying agent and the custodians—how do I give them 15 shoeboxes and go, well actually this is what I've got?"

You can't just wrap something in a certificate and call it investible. You need unified custody, transparent provenance, and a structure that traditional financial gatekeepers will accept. The solution required a regulated digital custodian—SECDEX—capable of connecting to the registries and projects and also providing a single home for these disparate assets with full blockchain-enabled transparency.

Professor Wilson wasn't just building a financial product. She was building an entire ecosystem. "I haven't just had to develop the tool, the financial tool, and get all the regulation components done. But we've actually had to go out to the market to partner with and find solutions to difficulties in the market."

The greater than two-year process involved assembling regulated counterparties for every function: issuer, strategy manager, paying agent, traditional custodian for liquid assets, and digital custodian for carbon assets. "Every single counterparty to the transaction is a financial service licensed regulated entity." She also engaged ratings agencies such as BeZero and Sylvera and carbon pricing and predictive modelling platforms such as MSCI, Clear Blue Markets, Bloomberg, S&P to establish institutional standards for the new asset class.

The infrastructure includes what Wilson calls "source to sale" provenance and transparency. All assets sit on the digital custodian, blockchain-enabled, with their investment grade attributes anchored to the blockchain. "They sit in one repository, and they never leave it. If the carbon credits are sold and offset by emitters using carbon accounting methods or we sell them on the secondary market, there's a direct pathway everybody can see. You can see the URL link, and you can actually hop in and physically see 100% the movement of that asset on the blockchain."

This addresses fundamental trust issues—greenwashing risks, double-counting concerns, lack of audit trails. The blockchain functions as the foundation of what Wilson calls "the trust layer" which is driven by the strengths of people, processes and technology working together.

Professor Wilson learned to separate two fundamentally different types of risk, using a deliberately simple metaphor.

"I used to say to them, just imagine a carbon credit is a brick. Forget that it's carbon, it's a brick. And if I have a whole warehouse full of bricks, I still have a process of de-risking. There's a process of de-risking the brick—where it's been made and produced and whether it's real and the quality of it. But there's also the second part, and that's the risk mechanism of the financial tool."

The distinction matters because different investors approach it differently. "If you're talking fine wine or diamonds, generally people ask about the asset before they ask about the process. But for institutional capital markets, they ask about the process and money flows first. So, if the process doesn't work, they're not interested in the asset."

This shaped how Wilson structured everything and even how she talks about it. Wilson deliberately shifted the language from "carbon credits" to "investment-grade carbon assets." The terminology is strategic. "Don't take people down a rabbit hole you'll never get yourself out of. Keep it where this conversation needs to be. It's a financial tool. It's got a return on investment. It's de-risked for investors."

Wilson calls this "de-emotionalizing" the conversation—removing climate impact from the pitch and focusing purely on growth and process. "I want to shift climate from the profit and loss sheet to the balance sheet. I want to turn this from being a cost to an investment class commodity. Take the emotion out of this and turn it into a financial product."

De-risking the process wasn't enough. Wilson also had to address asset quality in a way institutional investors would recognize. Her approach involves adding layers of third-party validation and attributes to the assets before acquiring them for the AMC and they enter the portfolio.

"We curate the assets and then we do something ex-post to create the attributes of an investment-grade asset." This includes ratings from independent firms like BeZero, Sylvera, and Calyx Global—assessments done with rigor, before assets are included. "No asset goes into the AMC unless it's had an ex-post or ex-ante rating. And we are targeting A-plus. So, we're taking the cream of the crop."

The approach also includes insurance wrapping and full digital provenance. "These are different layers of attributes that we've given to the investment asset. It's almost like getting a piece of gold and polishing it up. When you see a piece of gold out of the ground, it's dull. And so, we've literally taken these assets and done something very different to them to de-risk that space."

The curation strategy itself is sophisticated. Spot credits provide immediate exposure. Forward contracts with verified but not-yet-producing projects offer 50–60% discounts—like the Ghana Green Guard Programme producing at least 305 billion credits over 25 years. Article Six sovereign-to-sovereign agreements provide the highest credibility. And rights issuance programs—the deepest discounts of all—provide seed capital to sovereign-backed projects.

"Because they're discounted, when the assets are actually issued and go to market in two years time, we've got incredible growth that we're driving and performance."

At the Blue Economy Finance Forum in Monaco, Wilson discovered something unexpected about why traditional climate finance wasn't reaching projects that needed it most.

"When you talk to those who need the capital—small island nations for example—they said none of that money is actually available to them." The head of the small island nations alliance explained that collectively, these nations manage 73% of the ocean's marine parks. "They said the current money sitting in all these funds and bonds, it's not available to them. Most importantly, they also can't get seed and Series A capital to get projects going."

The structure Wilson had built solved this too. By buying assets rather than investing directly in projects, it sidesteps a fundamental obstacle. "The big banks just don't have the mandate to directly invest into a project, many of them who don't have a balance sheet to justify how the loans might be paid back."

But they can invest into a structured product within a regulated architecture that utilizes carbon as its investment universe. And when they do, capital flows back to projects in a new way. "I can take rights issuance from those projects. I can procure those agreements into the AMC. Investors invest and ultimately, I've provided the liquidity through a different tool directly back to those projects. But I've also given investors the greatest ability to maximize their exposure to the exponential growth of the assets without the downside risk."

Wilson calls this the virtuous cycle. Institutional investors get de-risked exposure to a high-growth uncorrelated asset class. Projects, especially in developing nations, get early-stage capital without requiring structures that aren't available to them.

"We overcome the challenge of direct project risk because we're actually just buying the asset and we only buy assets that have a certain attribute attached to them."

What started as a project to make carbon credits investible ended up creating an entirely new pathway for capital to reach climate projects. But it only worked because Professor Wilson spent two years building the infrastructure first—the custody solution, the regulatory relationships, the trust layer, the unified provenance system. Sometimes assetization isn't about wrapping something in a financial product. It's about building an entire ecosystem, so the wrapping becomes possible.

BRINGING DIGITAL ASSETS INTO THE FINANCIAL MAINSTREAM: NISHA SURENDRAN

This interview examines how institutional custody infrastructure bridges blockchain's 24/7 operations with traditional finance's business-day settlement windows. The discussion demonstrates the operational challenges of making digital assets genuinely bankable for regulated institutions—the unglamorous but essential plumbing that enables assetization.

Nisha Surendran is the Head of Digital Asset Custody at Citi, one of the world's largest financial institutions. A computer science engineer by training, she spent years working in traditional banking infrastructure—helping companies navigate global payments and the friction of moving money across borders. Around 2020, she discovered blockchain technology and the Bitcoin white paper, recognizing in them a parallel financial system that could solve problems she'd lived with for years. That realization led her to her current role, where she's helping Citi build the infrastructure to bring digital assets into regulated finance.

Custody may not be the most glamorous topic in finance, but it's arguably one of the most critical—especially when it comes to digital assets. Without secure custody infrastructure, tokenization remains theoretical. Surendran explains what makes digital asset custody fundamentally different from traditional custody using what she calls her "lockbox mental model": "The way I think about this is you've got a lockbox—think of a glass lockbox so you can see what's inside. It's got a number lock outside. The number lock is like the cryptographic key. Essentially, safekeeping assets in the lockbox boils down to safekeeping the cryptographic key that gives you access to that."

You can put anything of value inside a token—digital money, Bitcoin, Ethereum, digital securities, NFTs. More importantly from an assetization perspective, you can also use tokens to "containerize" off-chain assets (a process referred to as tokenization of real-world assets (RWA)). These could be equities, bonds, shares in real estate, fine art. Like securities, the token is an all-purpose container.

The lockbox is secure because of cryptography, but the critical point is safekeeping the key. As the saying goes in the crypto world: not your key, not your crypto. This is where institutional custody providers like Citi come in, applying the same operational rigor and risk controls to digital assets that they apply to traditional securities.

Making assets "bankable" means more than just holding them securely. As Surendran describes it, three things happen simultaneously: "First, you have them within the same rails that power all of the other assets. So now you can access them in a safe and sound manner—be it crypto assets, be it tokenized real-world assets." Second, they're brought into the AML and KYC compliance framework of regulated financial products. Third, "you apply the same level of operational and financial risk and controls to these products as is applied to other financial assets."

Once an asset is custodied within the regulated system, it stops being exotic or inaccessible. It can be held alongside equities and bonds, included in portfolio statements, used as collateral, or financed against. A tokenized art collection, properly custodied, could theoretically be used to borrow against—"as long as you find someone to value it, price it," Surendran notes. The technology enables the functionality; the rest is market infrastructure developing around it.

But she cautions against technological determinism: "I think sometimes as technologists or folks who are very into the digital asset and blockchain space, we have a tendency to wish away all of the other stuff. But I think technology can solve a part of the problem in terms of the 'how' of delivery. You absolutely need to start with the legal, contractual, the business case, and the framework for how this would work." Technology is necessary but not sufficient. Legal frameworks, valuation methodologies, and market-making infrastructure must all develop in parallel.

When it comes to which assets benefit most from tokenization, Surendran sees value creation as "barbelled"—concentrated at both ends of the liquidity spectrum. "At one side you have the highly liquid, high-velocity assets like tokenized money market funds where there's a lot of value in moving those quickly through the system and unlocking faster settlement times." At the other end are "the less liquid, less accessible assets, be it private assets, be it real-world assets where you're just solving for the fact that these assets do not have a financial infrastructure today. Everything in the middle has a reasonably functional infrastructure."

The middle of the market—publicly traded equities, standard bonds, mainstream securities—already works reasonably well. The real opportunity lies at the extremes: making ultra-liquid assets move at the speed of capital and making previously illiquid or inaccessible assets investible in the first place.

One challenge that doesn't get discussed much is interoperability—not between blockchains, but between blockchain infrastructure and traditional financial systems. "As a regulated institution, it is: how do you make the blockchain infrastructure interoperate with the traditional infrastructure? Because the seam where the traditional brushes up against the digital—that's where a lot of our work is going in right now." The technical complexity is substantial: traditional custody infrastructure uses static account structures at central securities depositories, while blockchain infrastructure operates with assets in addresses controlled by cryptographic keys that may rotate regularly. "So how do you map all of this ever-changing landscape of assets at different addresses to a static account structure on a traditional accounting system? That's the first-level problem."

Then there's the temporal mismatch: "Blockchain infrastructure is 24/7, it's always on," while traditional infrastructure is moving toward accelerated settlement but isn't there yet. "In simple terms, this means that you need to align your weekend availability, your green zones, to match and support the digital asset ecosystem as it stands today." This is unglamorous but essential work—building bridges, solving for the fact that blockchain doesn't sleep while traditional finance takes weekends off, mapping ever-changing wallet addresses to fixed account structures.

Beyond custody and basic transactions, programmability represents what Surendran calls "a second layer of unlock." Traditional finance has ways of creating programmable conditions—an escrow account is technically programmable—but "the power now though is you can build this logic directly into the settlement layer" using smart contracts. "Rather than having an application layer where you have the logic, then somebody triggers a workflow, and then you go and enforce that on an account—there's so many touchpoints, there's a lot of manual stuff to support programmability in the traditional world. But using blockchain smart contracts, you can just bake that right into the settlement layer."

Smart contracts also enable composability: "You can have one program, one smart contract, do a few things, trigger another smart contract that does a few things, so you can start building more complex financial products." Citi's first pilot use case in trade services replaced a letter of credit with a smart contract: "As the ship goes through a canal where you're making the payments at particular milestones, these are now automatically released via smart contract." This is where tokenization moves beyond simply making more assets accessible and begins to enable entirely new types of financial products—instruments with built-in logic, automated behaviors, and composable features that would be impossibly complex or expensive to implement in traditional systems.

ETHEREUM AND THE TREASURY REVOLUTION: JOE LUBIN AND JOSEPH CHALOM

This interview explores Ethereum as settlement infrastructure and the emergence of digital asset treasuries as a new corporate finance model. The discussion of staking yields, programmable money, and AI agents transacting on-chain illustrates how tokenization enables both capital appreciation and productive use of treasury assets—a combination unavailable in traditional reserve strategies.

Joe Lubin co-founded Ethereum and founded Consensys, one of the most influential companies in the blockchain space. Joseph Chalom is CEO of Sharplink and a former BlackRock digital assets executive who helped launch the first Ethereum ETF. Between Lubin's decade-plus building Ethereum infrastructure and Chalom's Wall Street pedigree, they offer unique perspectives on how institutional adoption of blockchain and crypto is actually unfolding.

In this conversation we explore the emerging digital asset treasury (DAT) model, what makes ether potentially superior to bitcoin as a reserve asset, what institutional adoption actually looks like on the ground, and the emerging tokenization infrastructure.

The conversation begins with an update on Ethereum, which had just turned ten years old. After a decade of building infrastructure, the mood in the ecosystem is bullish. "Ethereum's firing on all cylinders and keeps adding more really interesting cylinders," Lubin says. The network has been operational nonstop for all those ten years. More significantly, traditional finance is now onboarding to DeFi, ecosystem sentiment is very high, and regulatory headwinds have turned to tailwinds. "It is our mainstream moment."

Chalom, coming from twenty years at BlackRock where he spent the last five to six years leading digital assets, sees Ethereum as something fundamental. "When I think of Ethereum, I think of it as a new kind of decentralized public infrastructure. Something that essentially provides a settlement layer for all sorts of financial transactions, economic activity, and AI agents. And it's meant to be that collective connective tissue of the world economy." The motivation is practical: building a bridge between traditional investors and crypto finance. Not just the $4 trillion of digital asset market cap, but "the hundred trillion that will be tokenized."

But why the focus on finance first? When asked about non-financial use cases, Lubin gets to something fundamental about how the internet went wrong. The internet was built without two critical pieces built into it: identity and money. "And that caused the internet and the web to do some disturbing things. So essentially it ended up building out of the playbook of the 20th century, where the internet just became a gigantic mall, selling lots of stuff. And essentially it became an advertising and e-commerce machine. And it did end up turning into a weapon of mass manipulation."

By getting the money layer right first—where you can inspect everything, where you know explicitly what you're paying for—blockchain technology offers a chance to rebuild the foundation differently. So finance provides the necessary foundation.

Sharplink's story illustrates how quickly things are moving. The company is public and NASDAQ-listed. Historically, it focused on affiliate gaming businesses. Then in June of 2025, the company pivoted to become a digital asset treasury company.

Chalom joined as CEO in July of 2025 because he genuinely believes there's an Ethereum opportunity that's going to change the world. The logic is straightforward: if you believe that Ethereum is a long-term, multi-decade transformational technology, then it's a great time to buy ether, the token that secures that technology.

But it's not just about accumulation. "In the short to mid-term, if you accumulate billions and billions of dollars of ether, there are tremendous opportunities to both support the Ethereum ecosystem through providing that ether to bootstrap protocols, to create value for our shareholders. More importantly, over time to build new businesses. And these are businesses that will not only be Ethereum aligned but hopefully spin off Ethereum or ether-denominated revenue, and then you start a flywheel."

This perspective comes from experience. When Chalom was at BlackRock helping launch the first Ethereum ETF in July 2024, the team spent considerable time understanding the ecosystem and speaking to hundreds of investors. "I came to believe this is going to be the bridge between traditional finance and capital and this decade-long opportunity, which will be really rewarding for investors."

As a DAT, Sharplink represents something completely new: a publicly traded company that raises capital specifically to accumulate ether as its primary treasury asset, stake it to generate yield, and use that asset base to build aligned businesses.

The obvious comparison is Strategy. Michael Saylor, the company's founder and executive chairman, pioneered the concept of bitcoin as a treasury asset, and both Lubin and Chalom acknowledge his achievement. Saylor demonstrated that if you accumulate assets in a treasury, your company often trades at a multiple of the net asset value of your underlying treasury assets.

But ether as a treasury token has significant advantages over bitcoin. "Yes, you raise capital and buy ether primarily for long-term capital appreciation, similar to what you would do for bitcoin. But ether works for you. Bitcoin is a great store of value," Chalom explains. "The Bitcoin network does one thing exceptionally well, which is store and move bitcoin. Ethereum as a network—if you own the native token ether, you can stake it. You could do a lot of things in the ecosystem that drive yield, a baseline 3% yield. But in DeFi, as you go up a little bit on the risk curve, you can accumulate even more yield. And most of that would be treated as revenue in a public company. And so if you think about owning the ether, getting capital appreciation on top of that, getting a yield—that is actually a smarter and better treasury asset."

There's another advantage: "Because Ethereum has the opportunity and a community of developers and builders and applications, as a treasury company you can do incredible things to bootstrap, build businesses, to support that community." It's about participating in an ecosystem as much as about holding an asset.

For investors wanting exposure to ether, the options have evolved. Traditionally, you'd need custodial accounts, buy spot ether, figure out how to hold it safely, then stake it to get yield.

About a year ago, ether ETFs arrived, offering a familiar wrapper for institutions. But there's a catch: in the United States at the time of writing, the SEC hadn't approved staking for ETFs. And even when it does, ETFs face a structural problem. "You have an issue of daily liquidity, meaning those ETFs have to be able to satisfy daily redemptions. And when you stake ETH, you're in some staking and unstaking queue, which used to be measured in days, now is measured in weeks. So you're likely not going to be able to stake even 50% of your ETH if you're a responsible fiduciary," says Chalom.

A DAT solves this. Owning an ETH DAT gives you exposure to ether's capital appreciation without an asset manager fee, with the ability to stake 100% of the assets to earn yield. "Nearly a hundred percent of our assets are staked to date," Chalom notes.

The conversation shifts to tokenization and real-world assets. What makes Ethereum the infrastructure of choice?

Lubin describes Ethereum as decentralized and credibly neutral—an infrastructure that no minority set of actors can improperly manipulate. "It's the first implementation of rigorous, trustworthy infrastructure on the planet."

Chalom brings a traditional finance perspective. The current system is full of friction. "You have these intermediaries who play roles to try to move money, to move securities, to help in that exchange of value, but everything is delayed. Some assets settle T+1. If you look at loans, they settle T+20. You see people holding money over nights and weekends collecting rents, and what that does is create massive risks and friction in the ecosystem."

The beauty of tokenization goes beyond just putting things on a blockchain. "Instant settlement. Atomic settlement. Think of the risk and capital you take out of this inefficient, traditional financial ecosystem." Then there's composability: "Why can't you own the S&P 500 and lend it in a tokenized form? Why can't you exchange the S&P 500 for the NASDAQ QQQ fund? When you have on-chain transactions where you have complete composability and real time pricing of transactions that can settle instantly, the velocity of movement of money and transactions is going to increase."

Chalom sees another shift coming, and sooner than most expect: AI agents operating on Ethereum infrastructure.

Every industry is trying to adopt agentic workflows—using AI agents to handle tasks autonomously. They're doing it because of massive cost and labor pressure, realizing that many workflows can be handled through trusted or trustless agents. Chalom thinks Ethereum will become the transaction layer where AI agents interact with each other, not just for finance but across all kinds of workflows.

He points to proposed Ethereum standards that would allow AI agents to transact directly with each other on-chain, relying on identity and reputation systems built into the protocol. The boundaries and logic for what agents can do would be native to Ethereum rather than requiring separate off-chain systems. "I think not years from now, but much sooner, you'll start seeing each of us have AI twins or AI wallet twins who will understand your preferences and be able to execute on them, in your portfolio or in predictive markets or in how you govern parts of your lives."

He acknowledges that adding AI to the conversation often feels cliché but he's convinced the impact will be massive and underestimated. "People believe it's years away, and I think it's months away."

Lubin confirms this isn't speculation: "The AI agent economy is being built out heavily on Ethereum. So that registry of AI agent services is an Ethereum native construct."

IT'S THE (BANKING) NETWORK, STUPID: LUCAS ERETH

This interview argues that assetization derives its power from operating within traditional banking networks rather than replacing them. The discussion examines network effects, the practical advantages of existing financial rails, and why tokenization and securitization should be viewed as complementary approaches rather than competing paradigms.

L
ucas A. Ereth is a Member of the Board of GenTwo Digital, where the mission is closing the gap between traditional financial markets and emerging crypto markets. His path to that role winds

through California's tech hubs, where he built his career as a serial entrepreneur focused on digital media and venture capital. He was also a managing member at Forstmann & Company, where he had the privilege of working alongside J. Anthony Forstmann, the US hedge fund pioneer. But the turn that shapes his current thinking came in 2016, when he got into crypto. "As for digital assets specifically, I got into crypto in 2016 and I have always been a big believer in the space," Ereth says. That early conviction, combined with his tech-world instincts and deep finance experience, gives him a particular lens on assetization: he sees it not as a technological curiosity but as a play on the most powerful network effects in the global economy.

The conversation around tokenization and assetization often treats them as parallel innovations, two different approaches to similar problems. Ereth sees it differently. "Assetization and tokenization are similar," he explains. "They are both about putting wrappers around assets and letting them loose on a network. But by its very nature, assetization is far bigger than tokenization. That's because crypto runs on distributed ledger networks, and assetization on the existing banking networks. And these are far larger than crypto networks. For this reason, I think of tokenization as a subset of assetization, one of the several different types of wrappers that can be used as an output of the assetization process."

Tokenization has real advantages—automated transactions, enforceable contracts, reduced need for intermediaries. But there's a more fundamental consideration. "Being able to tap into the banking network with the securities that we are building through assetization is extremely powerful for digital assets," Ereth says. "Because guess what? The banking system is where the money is. So why not be there too? If you tokenize you can gain certain advantages, but from a purely asset-based perspective being only on a blockchain network also means limiting yourself to a certain audience."

The power of network effects is something the tech world understands instinctively. Ereth draws the parallel to consumer platforms. "The global banking system is an unfathomably large network. Or rather a combination of dozens of networks that are tied into each other. It is questionable if anyone has the complete overview, and there is massive complexity there. It's highly sophisticated, and in its way rather beautiful. And it all works. But many people still fail to appreciate the power of the network effects of the global banking system. Yet we see this power all the time in other contexts."

Take WhatsApp as an example. "It is practically unstoppable," Ereth says. "There are really only three things that can take it down. One is if the government intervenes and shuts it down for some reason. There is nothing anyone can do about that. Another is if there are technical glitches that disrupt service over a long time. Yet it's been estimated that if WhatsApp became unavailable or hard to use, it would still take a couple of months before users would finally switch to another network and not return to WhatsApp once it's fixed. And the third would be if a competitor showed up that was at least ten times better. But it's also been shown that even in this case, the new network would only have an about 3% chance of penetration in replacing the old, established one, despite being better."

Large networks are unstoppable because they compound. "The more people or institutions you add to a network, the more it accelerates, and the more unstoppable it becomes," Ereth explains. "Another great example is Uber. The more drivers you have in the network, the faster you can get a ride. So of course, you're going to choose Uber."

Financial infrastructure works the same way. "Same thing with WeChat. WeChat is an interesting one because it's similar to WhatsApp but they also settle transactions. Such private sector monopolies/networks are exactly what authorities in the world fear, so as not to lose control over the most powerful driver of the economy: money. My point though is that this same dynamic applies to banking networks. Look at SWIFT, for instance, which stands for Society for Worldwide Interbank Financial Telecommunications.

It is like the WhatsApp of banking. It is not going anywhere anytime soon because everybody knows it, understands it and uses it. Same with the International Central Securities Depositories (ICSDs) and all the other established agencies to settle financial transactions."

When asked if assetization gets its power from running on traditional rails, Ereth is emphatic: "Absolutely! That's what makes it so powerful. The securities we create can be held in existing bank accounts, transacted over the normal rails, and basically used in all the familiar ways. This has advantages for clients in terms of where they keep the assets, in terms of accounting, and in so many other ways. But it's not just better for clients. It's better for asset managers too, especially those being asked by their clients to handle certain types of alternative or non-bankable assets."

Ereth explains how this solves a problem for asset managers. "For one, we are creating these securities that run within the banking system so that everybody knows how to work with them. For asset managers, this also means they don't see the asset outflows. Because if you as an asset manager want to get your clients into alternative assets, if it's crypto or art or anything alternative, then you would most likely see an outflow of funds. You have to wire money to an art dealer to buy a Picasso or to a crypto fund to subscribe to an off-shore fund. And an asset outflow is something that hurts everyone in the respective financial services chain. It hurts the asset manager because the cash leaves the bank account. It hurts the bank too because they lose cash off their balance sheet. With assetization you don't have this problem because, while the assets are off-balance sheet and asset-backed, the security itself is still custodied in banks."

There are other advantages. "If you invest into an alternative asset, you often don't really have control of the underlying that you have invested in. I mean, yes, maybe in the Picasso example you get a painting that you can hang on the wall, but wouldn't it be nicer as an asset manager at least to have it still be part of your assets under management? Or you as the high-net-worth individual, the family office, or you as the end investor seeing it still in your bank account? Wouldn't that make things easier, not to mention ease your mind?"

Then there's reduced friction. "A traditional private placement is usually a ten-to-twenty-page document which everybody has to sign and then exchange, and there's lawyers and there's red tape going back and forth," Ereth says. "Now with assetization we are attaching an ISIN code, which in effect places the security in the global banking network, and then suddenly you can settle with a delivery versus payment transaction. This is extremely powerful, and very neat and efficient, especially for large amounts of money. And there is no KYC/AML necessary because all of that has already been carried out by the respective banks. And that can be a huge burden otherwise. Assetization transactions are bank-to-bank transactions. We are basically connecting you directly to the global banking system with minimal friction involved and with minimum hassle. And that's to me the winning formula here. There is just a great power in being able to transact within the traditional banking network."

This doesn't make crypto obsolete. "Quite the contrary," Ereth says. "As I mentioned, there are things you can do with crypto, or better said on blockchains, that you can't do as well in the traditional system. Programmability and instant settlement make blockchains very interesting payment rails for instance. I do believe that in five to ten years' time tokenization and digital assets will be so deeply integrated within the global banking system that they're basically a part of it. And then we can probably use sophisticated DLT protocols to settle transactions and tokenize real world assets. And we can make use of the power of blockchains. I think this is all coming, and we will use it without even realizing it's blockchain-enabled, which is exactly how it's supposed to happen. But in terms of the broader digital assets and DeFi space, I think the regulators will force all of that to become part of the traditional banking system, perhaps another network among all the others. And with assetization, we offer a bridge to that system already now, for example through securitizing digital assets and making them bankable."

Ereth sees a parallel between assetization and DeFi's democratization promise. "I would definitely agree" that assetization sounds like DeFi, he says. "I think that assetization will enable a radical democratization of finance that is akin to the DeFi dream. Consider access. Certain opportunities, often the most interesting ones, are not accessible to most investors. Only banks, qualified investors, and institutionals can partake in asset classes like private equity or hedge funds. With crypto for the first time ever in history, an asset class arose where retail investors had, so to say, first dibs on it. Mostly because institutional investors couldn't deal with it. And that was really cool, and I think a fair redistribution of some wealth out there. And now with assetization we are looking to make all assets accessible in a similar way. So we can now wrap up crypto and make it part of the banking system. And we can also assetize all the other non-bankable assets out there and give people access to them too and also create liquidity. And this will be done without banks as issuers and in a 1:1 asset-backed fashion similar to what DeFi is about."

The off-balance sheet structure makes this possible. Ereth explains the constraints banks face: "Historically, you could only securitize bankable assets like stocks and bonds, the things that banks can easily add and hold on their balance sheet. Now of course you can securitize more things too. But regulated banks have balance sheet restraints. So even if banks would want to issue exotic or alternative investment products, on crypto for instance, they would have to have massive amounts of reserve capital on their balance sheet. So that makes it just not viable and frankly, too expensive. And now with Basel IV coming, risk-weighted assets will require even more reserve capital on balance sheets."

The alternative changes the economics entirely. "With assetization we offer perfectly legal off-balance sheet vehicles that are 100% backed by the asset. That means that capital requirements don't apply, because they aren't necessary. These are not risk assets. And that in turn means anyone can issue these securities. You are freed from reliance on a bank and its balance sheet, though you are perfectly free to use the bank for custody and transactions. This also makes the system much safer. There is still the risk inherent in the underlying asset, of course. But these assets are by their nature ring-fenced. All of this will help usher in a more democratized global financial system, one that becomes fairer by the day."

THE ASSETIZATION OF PROFESSIONAL ATHLETES: PROFESSOR PIER-LUC NAPPERT

This interview examines human capital contracts in minor league base-ball, where players voluntarily become investible assets to fund their development. The discussion raises questions about the boundaries of assetization: when does turning people into financial instruments represent empowerment versus exploitation? The income-pooling and equitization models demonstrate alternative approaches to financing uncertain but potentially valuable careers.

Minor league baseball players face a stark reality: years of grinding poverty while pursuing million-dollar dreams. Most will never make it to the majors, yet they're locked into contracts that control their careers for up to a decade. Now, some are finding an unconventional solution—turning themselves into investible assets through financial contracts that would make a venture capitalist nod in recognition.

Pier-Luc Nappert knows this world intimately. An accounting professor at Quebec's Laval University, he spent a decade working in professional baseball, including seven years with the Quebec Capitals and three seasons with the Toronto Blue Jays. His academic research on what he calls "assetization in sports" reveals a fascinating paradox: players voluntarily seeking to become financial assets, not as exploitation, but as empowerment.

The economics of minor league baseball are brutal. Players sign with major league organizations at 18 or 21, receiving signing bonuses that range wildly—from $8 to 9 million for top prospects to as little as $1,000 for others. As Nappert explains, some players report receiving "a couple of baseball bats, a bag of chips and here's your plane ticket to get to Arizona or Florida."

Once in the system, players remain under organizational control for five to six years before reaching the majors, where the clock resets for another six years. "Only at 32 will you have the opportunity to become a free agent," Nappert notes. "At 32, most baseball players are declining. Their skills are greatly diminished. So there's not a lot of value left for these players."

During their minor league years, players historically earned around $10,000 annually—and only during the April-to-September season. "The rest of the year they need to work. They drive Uber, they work in restaurants. They teach baseball lessons to kids."

This creates a vicious cycle. Low-bonus players can't afford off-season training, coaching, or proper facilities—the very investments that might help them advance. Meanwhile, million-dollar prospects can hire personal coaches and train year-round. The system creates what Nappert calls a "winner-take-most dynamic, where you have a few players who will potentially make $100 million in their career, and the vast majority who will end up being released after three or four years in the minor leagues, and will never have an opportunity to play a single game in Major League Baseball."

Within this inequality, an interesting phenomenon emerged. Players began to notice that major league clubs were treating certain prospects as valuable assets—investing in their development, providing resources, managing their careers strategically. Following the Moneyball revolution, clubs started viewing players more explicitly as assets requiring investment and protection.

This created what Nappert terms "asset envy." Players understand the trade-offs. "They cannot necessarily move to another club. They cannot decide where they're going to play. But at least as assets they have opportunities. They have resources coming to them." Lower-tier players observed this treatment and wanted in. They wanted to feel valued by their organizations.

Financial firms recognized an opportunity. If clubs wouldn't invest in lower-tier prospects, perhaps outside capital would. These firms began offering what Nappert calls "human capital contracts" in two distinct models.

The equitization model works like venture capital for athletes. Firms evaluate talent, statistics, organizational fit, and injury risk, then make calculated bets on which players will beat the odds. "Based on their talent, the club they play for, their statistics at the minor league level or even in college, they try to forecast the probabilities that this player will become a major league player and how much earnings this player might get during his career."

The pitch is straightforward: "What if I give you $500,000 now in exchange for 5% of your future earnings?" Players assess whether the deal makes sense for them. Some decline—either because they've already received multi-million dollar signing bonuses and don't need the capital, or because they overvalue their own prospects, which is natural. But for low-bonus players, the calculation looks different.

"If you got $50,000 as a signing bonus, you may jump on this amount because you can invest it in yourself. You can stop working in the off-season. You can hire coaches. You can eat well. You can have your own apartment."

The structure is pure equity, not debt. "If the player after two years is released, the firm will not get anything out of it. So that's not a loan. That's an equity stake that the firm takes into a player's career."

The income pooling model takes a different approach. Firms "try to put similar value players together in a pool. What they agree is that they are going to share a certain percentage of their future earnings with the other members of the pool."

A pool might consist of 10–30 players considered to have similar prospects. "At time zero, everybody's considered to have similar kind of expected value, but as years pass by, some players become superstars and earn millions of dollars. Others will leave baseball with nothing left. You don't necessarily know what the actual value of your human capital is, but at time zero, everybody is valuable and you accept to share your potential upside to protect your downside."

The structure distributes risk in a way that individual contracts cannot. Players who succeed subsidize those who don't, but everyone benefits from upfront capital that improves their collective odds.

The income pooling model faces its own challenges. In theory, it's perfect for top prospects—several high-value players pooling risk knowing some will likely succeed. "If you put 10 of them in a pool, you're pretty sure that at least five are going to make a lot of money in their career. You don't know which five, but you know that some of them will."

But overconfidence and pride make these players resistant. "They don't want to believe that they might miss. They don't want to believe that they will not become superstars."

Lower-tier players embrace pooling precisely because they recognize their long odds. The problem is that a pool of 30 marginal prospects might produce zero major leaguers, leaving nothing to distribute. "It's very possible that nobody out of these 30 players are going to be major league players and make a lot of money. If you get one, that's good for everybody, but it's possible that no one will make money and there's not going to be any cash swaps eventually."

The market remains relatively small. Early attempts at retail investment—including a NASDAQ-listed company called Fantex that let fans invest in specific players—didn't gain traction. Current firms are privately held, backed by institutional investors and high-net-worth individuals.

But Nappert sees broader potential.

"I can see this model being applied to a lot of different industries or professions where there's a lot of variance in potential outcomes. Maybe artists, musicians, screenwriters, entrepreneurs—anyone in a field where a few succeed spectacularly while most struggle, but everyone needs capital to develop their skills."

The concept could theoretically extend to creating diversified pools that balance stable earners with high-risk, high-reward careers. As Nappert muses: "I'm a university professor. I am not going to make a million dollars a year. But I will have a decent income stream for the next 25, 30 years. I have a full pension. Could I pool my income with some high volatility people and say, okay, I'm going to be the bond in the portfolio?"

Nappert's work reveals something counterintuitive about assetization. "I totally understand the discomfort about talking about people in asset terms," he says. The connotations are troubling, historically linked to slavery and exploitation.

But the reality is more complex. Baseball organizations already treat players as assets, controlling their movement and careers for over a decade. Human capital contracts simply give players tools to benefit from that same logic. They can't escape being assets to their organizations, but they can become assets to themselves.

"To me it's mostly a mode of governance," Nappert reflects. "It's not necessarily about the semantics of it. It's really about how you manage things or, in my case, people, as assets. You can consider things to be commodities. You can consider people to be employees, but framing something as an asset is powerful, and it's performative in the sense that it creates something and it shapes how you view this thing and what you do with it."

For now, most players Nappert interviewed reported satisfaction with their arrangements, though he notes a crucial caveat: "The vast majority of players that I spoke with were not yet at the major league level, so they didn't have to pay back yet. Who knows what they are going to think about that in 10 years, when a significant portion of their earnings will flow back to investors or other pool members."

The experiment continues. Minor league players keep chasing their dreams, now with venture capital in their corner. Whether they'll look back on these deals as liberation or exploitation may depend entirely on whether they beat the odds—just like any other startup.

THE ACADEMIC STUDY OF ASSETIZATION: PROFESSOR KEAN BIRCH

This interview traces how assetization emerged as an academic field, beginning with intellectual property studies and expanding to natural capital, infrastructure, and data. The discussion examines what happens when previously non-financial domains—knowledge, ecosystems, personal information—become structured as investible assets, and how policy and national accounting standards shape these transformations.

When we started writing our first book on assetization, we did what any author does—we searched to see if anyone else had written about the topic. We found something unexpected: an academic book called *Assetization: Turning Things into Assets in Technoscientific Capitalism*, published by MIT Press in 2020.

The book, edited by Professor Kean Birch from York University in Canada and Professor Fabian Muniesa from Mines Paris-PSL, turned out to be something quite different from what we were doing—a collection of academic essays examining assetization from a scholarly perspective. Through social media, we connected with Birch and his colleagues and discovered that we were, in a sense, two sides of the same coin. As one of them tweeted: "We've written the theoretical book and they've written the practical how-to."

Since then, Birch has become a friend of GenTwo. He's visited us several times in Zurich, spoke at our AssetRush conference, did a terrace talk with us, and served on the jury of our Assetization Leaders List. This conversation was adapted from his appearance on our podcast.

We started by talking about the two different takes on assetization we have. As Birch put it: "I think there's a difference between the way academics see the world and a lot of practitioners see the world. We are taking things apart and trying to understand them, while practitioners are trying to put things together."

The academic interest in assetization has deeper roots than you might expect. Birch traces it back to the late 2000s and early 2010s, when intellectual property became a significant policy issue. "There was a lot of interest in intellectual property rights as an asset for startups in high tech sectors like the biotech sector, but also the implications of these intellectual properties for research, for knowledge production," he explains.

What triggered this wasn't just market activity—it was a shift in how governments measured economic activity.

"I think it starts emerging as a policy issue because policy makers were starting to think about research and development as a particular kind of asset. They started trying to change national accounting standards to incorporate R&D as an asset rather than an expense or expenditure."

When the OECD, World Bank, and IMF started publishing reports on intellectual capital and knowledge capital, it reflected a fundamental reframing of what knowledge could be and how to govern it.

The 2020 book that emerged from this interest covers a remarkable range of topics. At a 2016 conference in Barcelona, Birch and Muniesa put out a call for papers and were surprised by the response—over 30 proposals came in. The topics that emerged fell into four broad categories: knowledge, nature, infrastructure, and social assets.

The knowledge category includes work on intellectual property and patents, particularly in biotech. This research revealed some fascinating market dynamics. Many biotech startups don't have the capacity to develop all their innovations, so they fund their primary research by selling off IP for projects they won't pursue themselves. "That was a major financing route for them that provided them with capital," Birch notes.

The nature and environment category examines things like natural capital accounting—treating ecosystems as assets—and what that means for investment strategies. There's also work on oil wells, particularly relevant in a country like Canada with enormous numbers of wells.

Infrastructure studies include work on railways in Spain and on wind farms and solar panels in France. Birch says this is about the "different ways that you assetize the sun versus how you assetize the wind, what are the implications there, and how you have to organize it." The phrase captures something essential about assetization—turning natural phenomena into investible assets requires not just financial engineering but entire organizational frameworks.

The social category covers student loan debt and social impact bonds, "trying to influence social welfare policies through creating investible objects."

Since the 2020 book, the field has continued to grow. "We have over a hundred people who have signed up to a reading list listserv I've been organizing," Birch says. "There's plenty of people coming out with new research every day about assetization. It's getting some intellectual traction."

And just as changes to national accounting standards sparked interest in intellectual property fifteen years ago, history is repeating itself with data. "The UN Statistical Division has just produced its new System of National Accounts, which updated these national accounting standards to integrate digital data as an asset in national accounting. So there's a really interesting similarity in the periods of time. Now is another time when there could be another burst in interest in assets and assetization as a consequence of these policy activities."

Data has become Birch's primary research focus, and it's easy to see why. The rise of big tech companies and concerns about the data they collect has made this a major policy issue. But there's also a push to encourage the use of data in ways that create social benefits—responsibly and transparently. "On the one hand we really need to know who's collecting data, how valuable it is to them, because transparency ensures that we can try and hold people to account. On the other hand, we want to enable the aggregation of data to make better policy decisions, or better infrastructure decisions, or to build better products and services."

The challenge is breaking open what Birch calls "data enclaves"—the walled gardens where data is locked up—while ensuring it's used responsibly within privacy and data protection frameworks. This plays out differently across geographies. The United States has a fragmented, state-level regulatory approach. The European Union has taken a more integrated supranational approach with GDPR and a suite of acts—the Digital Markets Act, Digital Services Act, Data Act, and Data Governance Act. "These regulations and acts are frameworks for designing new kinds of markets—the markets that the EU wants them to be, not just simply a laissez-faire US kind of arrangement."

China has taken yet another path, with strong data localization regulations but also considerable experimentation. "They have been experimenting with data markets. Selling your own data. These are attempts to institute new kinds of markets." But these markets haven't taken off as expected, and Birch thinks he knows why.

The problem is what we might call the "$40 problem"—the value of an individual's data is tiny. "If an individual is going into a data market and saying, 'Hey, do you want to buy my data?' that data is going to be worth a pittance basically." This plays out even in court cases about data value, where judges see individual data points as having relatively minuscule value.

But if individual data has little value, collective data might be different. This has led Birch to think about data governance in collective terms—specifically, the concept of data wealth funds modelled on oil wealth funds. "If as individuals we cannot govern it ourselves, then collectively we can govern it. Put our data together, have a full database of all this information that is very useful to a lot of different institutions, governments, businesses. Just like an oil wealth fund, you charge for access and you use those returns to protect and support the wealth fund."

The revenues could fund technological solutions, address governance issues, and support social policies—all while ensuring collective control over a valuable societal resource. It's an elegant solution to the governance challenge of data assetization.

This is what makes the academic study of assetization valuable. Practitioners like us are focused on building—creating new investment products, bringing assets to market, solving immediate problems. Academics are studying the broader patterns, the unintended consequences, the governance challenges, and the policy frameworks that make assetization possible or problematic.

"For us, our starting point was the academic debates," Birch explains. "We were trying to differentiate what we saw as being different about capitalism today that wasn't coming through in the terms and terminology that other people were using. Assets and the asset form help us to do that by thinking about the transformation of things into this kind of capitalizable property that really changes the way we understand the economy, understand society, and understand the shifting governance frameworks."

We're not trying to win the same game. We're playing complementary ones. Practitioners build; academics analyze. We create new possibilities; they examine implications. We move fast; they think deeply. Both perspectives are essential to understanding the assetization revolution we're living through.

HOW GENTWO DIGITAL SOLVES INSTITUTIONAL CRYPTO'S ACCESS PROBLEM: MARK ARASARATNAM

This interview explains how off-balance-sheet securitization structures enable institutions to gain crypto exposure without Basel III capital requirements. The discussion demonstrates how existing regulatory frameworks can be satisfied through proper legal architecture, allowing traditional institutions to participate in digital asset markets without prohibitive balance sheet constraints.

T he crypto industry loves talking about bridges. Everyone wants to be "the bridge between TradFi and DeFi," as Mark Arasaratnam puts it. But most haven't actually built one. GenTwo Digital has.

Arasaratnam leads GenTwo Digital, the firm's digital assets arm. His path to crypto came through traditional markets—starting as a high-frequency equity trader before moving to FX, global macro, and entrepreneurial ventures in ad tech. Most recently, he was co-head of digital assets at Marex, a global brokerage, where he created structured products linked to crypto. Now he's in Zurich, applying GenTwo's proven securitization platform to crypto's institutional access problem.

The challenge is real. Despite Bitcoin ETFs, regulated custody solutions, and dozens of Swiss banks now able to hold digital assets, traditional institutions still struggle to get meaningful exposure. The barriers aren't technical anymore—they're structural.

When financial institutions want to enter the digital asset space, they face what Arasaratnam calls "the three C's": compliance, complexity, and custody.

"Compliance is a bit nebulous because right now the world is still trying to figure out where it fits into the digital asset space, and governments are trying to figure out how to navigate that. It gets complex. People are hiring whole teams of lawyers to figure this out. Countries have created proverbial sandboxes to test new paradigms, but a global standard is far from being ratified."

The operational complexity runs deeper than regulatory uncertainty. "From a settlement perspective, blockchains are fundamentally different to the way traditional assets settle. Traditionally, you have cash, equity, fixed income, and FX on different rails, and for the first time you have them all on the same rails. It's fundamentally different by design. That makes it complex because we're not used to settling those kinds of securities, because we have spent the last hundred years working on regular asset classes, crafting laws around an old way of thinking."

Custody has evolved considerably but remains challenging. "Custody has been difficult in the early years of crypto, and now institutions are becoming a lot more savvy in terms of with whom they want to be interacting." The good news is that bigger players are entering—regulated solutions like Zodia, a subsidiary of Standard Chartered, or Sygnum Bank in Zurich, or Amina in Zug. "It will also become a very low margin business because regulation will drive the way custody solutions are built from a technology perspective and from a compliance perspective. The same thing happened in TradFi. Differentiating will depend on added services and yield opportunities."

But there's a fourth barrier that often proves decisive: capital requirements.

Under Basel III regulations, holding crypto on a balance sheet can require risk-weighted asset reserves of up to 1,200%. That's not just expensive—it's prohibitive. "These prudential requirements make it almost impossible to deal in crypto," Arasaratnam explains. "Anyone who has crypto on the balance sheet will think, 'oh this is getting expensive.'"

This is where GenTwo Digital's approach diverges from the usual attempts to make crypto more accessible.

"We are able to create securitized vehicles that make it easier for institutions to get into the space. GenTwo as a company has been securitizing assets—all kinds of assets—for the last seven or eight years, from buildings to art funds to wine to any esoteric asset class, funds, derivatives, private equity funds, trackers, hedge funds. This is the bread and butter in terms of what we do. We've already created the legal structures for this stuff, and we've created the actual financial engineering backdrop for all these strategies. So digital assets was something we could bolt on fairly easily to cater to client demand."

The key is creating truly off-balance sheet structures. "These SPVs are done to move things completely off-balance sheet and be bankruptcy remote. If something happens to the main entity, nothing happens to the assets in custody, and that's an important part of it." Each vehicle has independent directors and a trustee based in Liechtenstein, ensuring complete separation from the issuing institution.

For end investors, this structure provides an additional benefit: full collateralization. The assets backing the certificate are held separately, protected even if the issuing institution fails.

Beyond access to spot exposure, institutional demand is moving systematically up the risk and yield spectrum. "We moved on from tokenized cash (USDT by Tether, USDC by Circle), to money market funds to private credit. So we're going from non-yielding pure cash to money market funds with some yield, and now to private credit. We're going up the risk curve, which is both a function of macro and Lindy effects. Tokenized cash has been proven, so why not tokenize other assets?"

GenTwo Digital recently launched a bitcoin accumulator with a crypto derivatives OTC broker based in the US and UK. This type of product is very common in traditional finance. "The OTC desk is very good at pricing volatility, hedging, and creating complex payoff structures. They manufacture the derivatives, and they are able to use our structures to wrap it into a security that is investible and bankable (not OTC). So an off-balance sheet structure with an ISIN attached to the security."

The model is attracting attention. "We're seeing more demand from other crypto derivative brokers who are coming to us and saying, 'how do we do the same thing?'"

Tokenization represents another frontier. "We don't have a global standard for native issuance on chain just yet. Yes, there are sandboxes, but they are just that—ringfenced tests. Switzerland has come a long way with its DLT act and other countries are slowly following suit. I think we will get there at some point, but right now we're still working through our existing compliance structures, and for that you need to segregate your assets into a vehicle and then you can tokenize the vehicle itself." GenTwo can create the certificate and work with tokenization engines to tokenize the product itself. "You can have tokenized Tesla or Google shares, for example, or a basket of Tesla, Google, and Nestle. That makes it super interesting because then you can have 24/7, T+0 settlement. Soon we will see tokenized private equity."

Switzerland's crypto infrastructure continues to develop in interesting ways. "There are dozens of banks in Switzerland that can custody digital assets," Arasaratnam notes. "If they're able to do derivatives, then structured products become a no brainer. They can offer that to their clients as well. We've got a lot of crypto native banks who are actually coming to us and asking us if they can do that in an off-balance sheet fashion."

The exchanges are also maturing. "They're becoming a lot more legitimized, and they're actually going more vertical. Look at what's happening with OKX. They received a MiCA license. Kraken secured a MiFID license in the EU. This is happening across the board for a lot of the largest liquidity players in the market. It makes it easier for them to work with regulated financial institutions so they can run the gamut from staking to spot liquidity to derivatives as well."

Looking ahead, Arasaratnam sees considerable momentum driven largely by regulatory clarity emerging from the US. "We're going to see a lot of regulatory compliance coming out of the US and I believe it's going to affect the industry in a momentous way. For example, we now have stablecoins that are functionally separate from securities (under the SEC) vs commodities (under the CFTC)."

But he's pragmatic about decentralization's ultimate role. When asked whether the masses truly want full decentralization, his answer is candid: "I think people have gotten accustomed to the workings of their financial institutions—if they make a bad transaction using a bank or something happens—transactions can be reversed. Having a decentralized blockchain will not allow you to do that. And that becomes tricky. I think people want the decentralized nature of it until something bad happens to them."

This points to blockchain functioning as an additional rail, additional infrastructure with genuine advantages, rather than a wholesale replacement of existing systems. "We're seeing a shift from what's happening in DeFi to mimicking what's happened in TradFi, from tradable yields to baskets to every kind of asset. There are even structured products on chain. So is there a demand for these issuances natively on chain? We don't know yet. The market is still finding its feet."

What's clear is that institutional adoption doesn't require institutions to become crypto-native. They just need familiar securities with ISINs that work within existing systems—securities that happen to provide exposure to digital assets without the regulatory headaches or capital charges. GenTwo Digital has built that bridge. Now the traffic is starting to flow.

URANIUM, AMCS, AND THE GREEN METALS INVESTMENT OPPORTUNITY: PATRICK MICHAELS

This interview examines commodities and mining equities through the lens of physical ownership and active management. The discussion of uranium storage, copper supply constraints, and ESG considerations in mining demonstrates how actively managed certificates can provide exposure to physical assets and specialized markets that passive vehicles struggle to access efficiently.

Mining and metals may not have the cachet of Silicon Valley start-ups or headline-making art auctions, but for Patrick Michaels, Executive Chairman of Zuri-Invest, they're the unseen bedrock of the modern world—and the next frontier in asset innovation. His approach fuses hands-on curiosity with Swiss finance tradition, marrying hard-hat practicality with bespoke financial engineering to unlock value in one of the world's oldest and most tangible industries.

Zuri-Invest's roots run deep. Founded as a family business over four decades ago, its original focus was classic discretionary asset management—a world of blue-chip stocks and conservative, risk-balanced portfolios. Michaels, who joined the firm in 2003 in the second generation, came in with a passion for stock picking but soon discovered that true competitive advantage lay elsewhere. "My father introduced me to mining as an additional specialization to traditional investments," he says. "You always need some kind of an edge versus the usual blue chip ideas."

The company's evolution tracked the sector's own rollercoaster fortunes, but Michaels saw opportunity where others saw risk: "If you can't grow it or catch it, it comes from a dark hole in the ground. . . In our everyday lives we don't really appreciate what mining provides us and enables us as benefits and luxuries and necessities. Everything from phones and tools to the glass you drink from is a product of mining."

What distinguishes Michaels isn't just his background or sector focus, but his deeply tangible, almost tactile approach to investment. He doesn't just talk about metals—he brings them to meetings: natural uranium samples, dense copper nuggets, even a chunk of a gold-copper drill core. "This is copper through and through," he says, hefting the heavy metal. It's not for effect, but to remind his interviewer of the physicality—and reality—of what's at stake.

This hands-on attitude extends to due diligence. For every blue-chip mining stock or physical commodity Zuri-Invest considers, the firm undertakes real-world investigations: site tours of mines, in-person assessment of operations, and meetings with not just CEOs, but the frontline staff, probing the culture and efficiency of a company as much as its annual reports.

Mining's reputation often precedes it—risk, volatility, and, in the age of environmental consciousness, deep questions of impact. Michaels is well aware. ESG (environmental, social, and governance) factors are central to Zuri-Invest's screening: "No shortcuts on safety or community work. When we do our evaluation, if it's possible, we visit the production site. We want to see how happy the people are, how efficient they're set up. Are they ready for the next wave of competition?"

Responsible mining, he argues, isn't just a moral stance but a performance filter. Companies that manage their communities and employees well tend to deliver steadier returns and weather regulatory changes. "The good companies have kind of done the ESG approach since decades," he notes, insisting that these considerations are not new, but newly visible and scrutinized.

Transforming mining investments into modern, accessible assets requires more than sector expertise; it demands financial innovation. That's where the Actively Managed Certificate (AMC) comes in: "With AMCs, it's much easier to offer something to a qualified audience. We have our slogan: invest together with us. We always put our own money where we speak."

AMCs allow Zuri-Invest to securitize diverse baskets of hard-to-access assets: themed global mining portfolios, niche strategies (even a Greek equities basket), or, most strikingly, direct exposure to physical commodities, such as uranium. The flexibility of an AMC means that, within as little as three weeks, a tailored, compliance-ready investment vehicle can be crafted to client preferences—a process far swifter (and less costly) than traditional fund creation.

AMCs are also fundamentally modular. An individual investor, family office, or even a collaborative group of asset managers looking to specialize in an underexplored theme—say, rare earth metals or Mexican silver—can partner with Zuri-Invest to spin up a new AMC suited to their niche.

Nowhere is this innovation more apparent than in the company's uranium AMC, a product that allows investors to own a share of non-enriched, safely stored uranium—yellow powder bought and stored with Canada's leading uranium specialist. For most, investing in such a commodity would be off-limits due to storage, regulation, or lack of expertise. But in partnership with GenTwo, Zuri-Invest's structure has democratized exposure to an asset once reserved for industrial giants and utilities.

The appeal of passive, index-based investing is obvious for mainstream equities, but Michaels is convinced that, for mining and specialized markets, active management carries enduring—and perhaps growing—advantages. "If you're working in these special themes, like smaller markets or thinly traded mining shares, you really need to follow them carefully. If tomorrow the law changes in a mining country, you have to take a decision quickly. That's usually an advantage versus passive ETFs."

Monitoring regulatory, political, and supply risks is a full-time job. Mining markets are prone to disruptions—tax policy changes, permitting delays, or sudden shifts in global demand can upend portfolios overnight. "You need agility, and that's where a truly actively managed AMC can deliver something the passive guys can't."

Today's "green economy"—trillions spent on renewable infrastructure, electric vehicles, and grid upgrades—is ultimately powered by old-economy metals. Michaels points to copper as critical: "Copper is the heart of electric vehicles, the key part in data centers and the global energy grid. But are there enough new discoveries to replace even current depletion? The answer is no."

Nuclear and copper together frame his view of the energy transition. For him, uranium is not a side bet but a core enabler of decarbonization because it delivers clean, always-on power in a way that intermittent renewables cannot. As he puts it, "If we are serious with the CO_2 targets, you cannot do it only with solar and wind. . . you need something that runs 24/7 with very low emissions, and that is where nuclear and uranium come in."

Copper plays a similarly pivotal role on the demand side. Michaels calls it "the metal of electrification" and "the heart of the electric motor," stressing that every new electric vehicle, charging station, data center and upgraded power line is effectively "a copper story." At the same time, he warns that "the big, long-life copper mines are depleting" while "it takes longer and longer" to permit new projects as environmental and social standards tighten and opposition grows.

This mismatch between soaring need and constrained supply is what turns uranium and copper into strategic "green metals" rather than just another commodity cycle. "Electricity demand is growing every year," he notes, pointing to forecasts and industry talks that call for hundreds of billions in annual grid investment, "and almost all of that depends on more copper and, in many countries, more nuclear." For Michaels, that combination of structural demand, physical scarcity and political complexity is precisely why these markets call for active management and carefully structured AMCs, not just passive exposure.

By transforming mining and commodities into accessible, bankable AMCs, Michaels and Zuri-Invest are offering professional investors a way to reconnect with the foundational realities of the economy. In a world awash in abstract financial products and digital assets, the elemental, tangible value of metals remains a source of security, growth, and, increasingly, innovation.

"For us, it's about putting together expertise, relationships, and new structures. AMCs allow for agility, diversification, and full transparency for investors who want to benefit from what's below the surface, literally and financially."

Michaels' vision is not about riding commodity booms or speculating on the next headline. It's about steady, responsible value creation—and about remembering, in a digital age, the physical foundations on which the future is being built.

THE WORLD'S LARGEST LEGAL INSIDER MARKET: PASCAL SCHNEIDINGER

This interview explores how blue-chip art becomes investible through off-market sourcing, fractional ownership structures, and professional storage infrastructure. The discussion of information asymmetry, authentication, provenance, and the role of specialized expertise demonstrates both the opportunities and challenges of assetizing illiquid, high-value tangible assets.

When most picture the art world, they imagine glittering auctions, secretive collectors, and walls adorned with priceless works far out of reach for average investors.

Pascal Schneidinger's journey into this realm didn't start with a passion for Monet or a degree in art history. Instead, it began in Zurich, ran through New York's finance scene and Shanghai's retail industry, and ultimately converged in a mission: to turn some of the world's rarest paintings into a new, accessible asset class for a wider circle of investors.

Schneidinger's resume includes stints in investment banking, real estate private equity, and entrepreneurial ventures in China, where he ran furniture and homeware stores for nearly a decade. Upon leaving China, he returned to Switzerland and spent two years in deep research, seeking a new, impactful business idea. He zeroed in on the art market not because he was an art insider—he wasn't—but because he saw the same characteristics that delivered opportunities in real estate: tangibility, inefficiency, and a stark lack of transparency.

"I always call it the largest legal insider market that exists," Schneidinger says of the art market. Unlike financial markets, where data and access are democratized, art is opaque. "If you're truly an insider, you simply have more information than people who are not in the market, and this information asymmetry creates advantages. . . If you're in a truly efficient market, what's your edge? You really don't have one in the long term. But the art market rewards those with access, information, and connections."

Having identified the market's inefficiency and access gaps, Schneidinger moved to build something that would bridge those divides—for himself, for investors, and for the broader financial marketplace.

The art market is not one homogenous entity but a world of segments, risk levels, and wildly varying value drivers. "Ninety to ninety-five percent of art you should only buy for emotional or cultural reasons," Schneidinger cautions. "But if you want to invest, you focus on the absolute top segment."

His firm, Partasio, targets a shortlist of about 40 "blue-chip" artists—creators whose work appears in major museums worldwide, whose auction records are robust, and who are globally relevant in the United States,

Europe, and Asia. These artists, exclusively post-1945 painters, represent the most stable, liquid, and least volatile investment profile in the art world.

"We want low volatility, good risk-adjusted returns, and long-term relevance. We are not in the business of speculating on the 'next big thing' in emerging art," he explains.

What distinguishes Partasio from other art investment schemes isn't just selectivity; it's method. All acquisitions are made "off-market," meaning no purchases at auctions, no buying from fairs, and, crucially, no acquiring works that have previously traded publicly. This strategy accomplishes two things: it gives Partasio access to unique, in-demand paintings before they face open competition, and it enables the company to negotiate purchases at significant discounts.

"If I can get access to a painting, so can many others. The more people look at something, the less pricing power you have," says Schneidinger. Sourcing is managed by a network of art market veterans, now his partners, whose decades of relationships open doors in what remains an intense relationship-driven business. The company evaluates each piece using both public sales data and private "insider" information, blending analytics with market intel unavailable to casual investors.

As he explains it, the research process combines data from the 50% of the art market that is public—mostly auction records—with information about the other 50% that changes hands privately. Public records provide a baseline for pricing, liquidity, and trends, but Schneidinger's team layers on the extra 10–20% of market intelligence available exclusively to long-standing insiders: knowledge of discreet buyers and sellers, the frequency and context of particular deals, and shifts in appetite across different regions. This blend of hard data and soft intelligence is what allows Partasio to treat each painting not simply as a cultural asset, but as a bankable financial product.

Schneidinger recognized that making art an accessible investment wasn't just about finding and buying great works—it was about structuring those investments so they could fit into modern portfolios. Working with platform and product specialists, Partasio created an Actively Managed Certificate (AMC), a financial product that pools fractional ownership of four to six selected paintings.

"With the AMC, the entire process is similar to buying shares or bonds. You invest through your bank, you see your investment in your custody account, and everything is handled securely and transparently," he says. The minimum investment is intentionally low by industry standards, making blue-chip art available to qualified investors who would otherwise be excluded by price and network.

Each portfolio is constructed to balance risk, achieve diversification, and offer timely liquidity upon sale of the works, which typically happens over a five-year period. As each painting is sold from the portfolio, proceeds are distributed directly back to investors according to their proportionate stake.

For now, Partasio's distribution strategy is firmly institutional. Rather than chasing retail investors directly, Schneidinger works through independent asset managers, family offices, and private banks that already sit at the center of clients' asset-allocation decisions. For these intermediaries, art is not a lifestyle purchase but another building block alongside equities, bonds, private markets, and real estate—albeit one that is currently underrepresented. "In most portfolios, the allocation to art is effectively zero," he notes, arguing that a small, carefully constructed slice—on the order of a few percent—can improve diversification without materially increasing risk.

While private individuals represent an obvious second distribution channel, it's one the firm has not yet pursued, since direct outreach to individual investors requires broad-based marketing resources and brand-building that Partasio does not currently have at scale.

As Schneidinger tells it, most investors don't understand the art market's supply and demand drivers, pricing mechanisms, or risk profiles.

Education is, therefore, a core pillar for Partasio. The company provides weekly market reports, hosts tours and expert events, and produces content to demystify the art market and connect investment decisions to both cultural and financial outcomes.

Schneidinger has noticed that his investor base falls into two main buckets: "pure financial investors" who seek return with minimal interest in the art itself, and "intellectually curious investors" who want both financial returns and cultural engagement.

All investors receive mini versions of purchased paintings, creating a tangible connection to the assets behind their capital. "When you make an investment decision, you have to be rational and objective. But once you've bought the painting, then you can really enjoy the cultural and emotional aspects. That's the best part about investing in art."

Every painting in a Partasio portfolio is stored in state-of-the-art, climate-controlled facilities in Switzerland, insured and protected as securely as gold reserves. Investors may visit their paintings at the warehouse or see them in curated exhibitions. While few have yet exercised this option, Schneidinger emphasizes the importance of transparency and access.

"These are not abstract financial instruments. They're physical, tangible works—sometimes objects of immense beauty and history—that happen to represent a strong store of value and potential return."

In today's market, blue-chip art performs a distinct role: capital preservation for the ultra-wealthy, alongside assets like gold and high-quality real estate. Schneidinger expects the market to remain "boring—but in the best way" for this segment, insulating investors from volatility and offering steady inflation resistance.

Trust is also foundational for both sides of the equation. Investors must trust that purchases are prudent, prices fair, and works legitimate with clear provenance. Sellers, meanwhile, must trust the discretion and financial solidity of buyers in a clubby, risk-averse community.

Perhaps the most profound change Partasio represents is not technological or financial, but philosophical. For centuries, access to rare paintings—and the financial benefits of their appreciation—was reserved for the super-rich and well-connected. By blending modern finance with art world savoir faire, Partasio welcomes both the experienced investor seeking diversification and the art lover who never imagined owning a share of a major masterpiece.

Partasio aims not just to unlock an asset class, but to open minds—showing both the art and finance worlds what's possible when two cultures learn to speak each other's language.

INDEX